This book is dedicated to my wife Miriam, HaShem's great encourager for my soul, and my sons, Josh & Matt, who have Messianic foundations established in their lives.

Note to the reader:

*Throughout the text, the Hebrew name "Yeshua"
is used normally for Jesus.
The name "Jacob" is also used for references to
the name and book of James.*

"Messianic Foundations"
by Sam Nadler
Copyright © 2010 by Sam Nadler
Word of Messiah Ministries
All rights reserved.
Printed in the United States of America

ISBN-13: 978-1534877771

MESSIANIC FOUNDATIONS

Fulfill Your Calling In the Jewish Messiah

SAM NADLER

Word of Messiah Ministries
2010

Table of Contents

Forward 6

Part One: God's Calling for Messianic Jews

1. God's Everlasting Love.................................. 11

    Good News Principles: *Tikkun Olam*................ 18

2. To the Jew First?.. 19

    Good News Principles: *Kiddush HaShem*........... 32

3. The Necessity of Messianic Congregations.......... 33

    Good News Principles: *Am Yisrael Chai*............ 41

4. The Faith of Our Fathers............................... 43

5. Faith in Yeshua Alone Saves.......................... 57

Part Two: God's Calling for Messianic Gentiles

6. The Gentile Great Commission....................... 77

7. Their Own Olive Tree 95

8. The Fullness of the Gentiles 109

9. Our Messianic Unity 127

10. Jewish Good News for Gentiles 133

Part Three: God's Calling for a New Covenant Messianic Faith

11. New Covenant Orientation 149

12. New Covenant Provisions 163

    (New Covenant and Kashrut (Food Laws))., ... 171

    (Shabbat in New Covenant Torah) 177

    (Circumcision and Gentiles) 181

13. Mature Faith 191

Selected Bibliography 204

Scripture Index 205

Forward

I live in a Messianic world. True, I am also an American, and so I have a great deal of freedom. Yes, I'm Jewish and seem to enjoy all things Jewish as a matter of personal preference, if not calling. Indeed, I'm a follower of Messiah Yeshua, and love to be around those who revere Him. Yet, all told, I live in a Messianic world, a world where my faith in Yeshua is freely expressed in a decidedly Jewish frame of reference.

I wrote this book to testify to the faithfulness of God. My heart's desire is not only to see Jewish people come to faith, but to see Jews and Gentiles become disciples of Yeshua, who is God's faithfulness to Israel. I believe Messianic congregations embody the testimony of God's faithfulness to Israel.

However, considering the difficulties facing our growing movement, our congregations need to be based on sound teaching. Sound teaching will give the wisdom, discernment, servanthood, substance, and focus which is vital for a Messianic movement. Without sound teaching on foundational matters—rooted in Yeshua and the Word—the Messianic movement will disintegrate and fall apart. If maturity as a witness-people is what we are after, sound Scriptural teaching is the only way to get there.

I am thankful for feedback from friends, leaders, and scholars: Seth Postell, Dan Gruber, Howard Silverman, Barney Kasdan, Vladimir Pickman, Barry Leventhal, Daniel Nessim, Barry Rubin, Michael Rydelnik, Steve Weiler, Jhan Moskowitz, Arnold Fructenbaum, David Taylor, and many others.

I thank my son Matt, who meticulously edited the manuscript, believing that this teaching is essential for the body of Messiah in general, and especially the Messianic movement.

I'm forever thankful for my wife, Miriam, an ongoing encouragement to me and my partner in ministry.

I'm thankful for the creative and diligent service of Natalia Fomin, who managed the design and layout of the book.

There are numerous others who spent many hours faithfully editing, proofing and serving in various ways, especially Ann Thomas, Pat Campbell, Greg and Marianella Leekley, Natalie Howell, Rosanne Howell, Ruth Zwicker, Stephanie Thompson, Joshua Spurlock, and Henn Hetzroni.

For these (and others I may have inadvertently overlooked), I say "Thank you, Lord!"

Sam Nadler, September 15, 2010

Part One

God's Calling for Messianic Jews

O Israel, hope in the Lord

From this time forth and forever.

Psalm 131:7

1

God's Everlasting Love

"At that time," declares the Lord, "I will be the God of all the families of Israel, and they shall be My people." Thus says the Lord, "The people who survived the sword found grace in the wilderness— Israel, when it went to find its rest."

The Lord appeared to him from afar, saying, "I have loved you with an everlasting love; Therefore I have drawn you with lovingkindness." (Jeremiah 31:1-3)

When Jeremiah wrote the above words, Israel had grievously sinned against the Lord and was sent into slavery in Babylon (606-536 BCE). This sending of Israel into captivity foreshadows a future tribulation period, called "the time of Jacob's distress" (Jeremiah 30:7).

The Hebrew word for "distress" is *tsara*, which can mean "trouble," or "tribulation." (From this, we also get the Yiddish word *tsuris*.) "At that time," seen from the previous chapter, Israel was pictured coming out of a horrific period, and into the Messianic Kingdom era (Jeremiah 31:1).

In the New Covenant, we see a similar picture of the pig pits and its effect on the prodigal son: he came to his senses and back to his father (Luke 15:16-17). Chastening comes in order to bring people back to God.

11

This "time of Jacob's distress" will take place *be'acharit hayamim*, in the last days (Jeremiah 30:7, 24). Why does this period occur?

1. To prove that Satan is a liar—he can't protect his own from the wrath of God (2 Thessalonians 2:3-12; Zechariah 3:1-3).
2. To punish the nations for their sins, especially the sin of anti-Semitism (Isaiah 29:7-8; Zechariah 14:16; Matthew 25:40, 45).
3. To prepare Israel for the returning King Messiah and Messianic Kingdom (Deuteronomy 4:30; Hosea 3:5; Zechariah 12:10).

It is this last reason that our section is primarily concerned with, though the second reason is considered as well (Jeremiah 30:8, 16, 20).

If you were God, what would you say to a people about to go into exile, to be removed from the place of blessing because of their disobedience? Would it be "I told you so," like a mother scolding her child when he catches a cold, for not wearing boots in the snow? Not so with our God. He gives Israel words of encouragement, even as they endure the just consequences of their unbelief.

In Jeremiah 31:1, we see that despite the captivity and tribulation pictured in Jeremiah's time, not even the future, greater Tribulation would end God's promises to Israel (Matthew 24:15-34). In fact, that period would be used to restore His people nationally to Himself: "all the families of Israel will be my people." This is the only place where such a precise promise is made. It is what Paul echoes in prophecy as well: "and thus all Israel will be saved" (Romans 11:26).

God's character is love. The Messianic Jewish movement, if it is of God, must be motivated by the reality of His love. However, instead of being a mere concept in the abstract, God's character is to be seen the way God revealed it. In the narrative of the Scriptures, God's love for the world and for repentant sinners, is based upon His love for a specific people: Israel. Let us look more closely at the final verse of the passage, considering three things revealed about God's love (Jeremiah 31:3).

GOD'S LOVE IS PERSONAL

God chose Israel by His sovereign love, and by this love He keeps Israel (Deuteronomy 7:6-8). Likewise, He chooses you and keeps you by that same love as well. It seems so simple: God loves you. Yet this is perhaps the most profound reality of the Bible. The God of the universe is not indifferent to who you are; rather He infinitely wills your good. He has a personal concern for you and each person in this world. This is the whole significance of the Good News of the New Covenant, and the only explanation for the sacrificial death of Messiah Yeshua. God didn't just send some messenger boy to tell us of His love, but rather, He Himself came in the flesh to demonstrate this love to us all (John 3:16; Romans 5:6-8).

To God, love is a personal matter. The Hebrew word for "loved" is *ahav*—a deep desire which reflects God's heart. Even as He demonstrated that love personally, we are to respond personally to Him, by personally trusting in Yeshua and personally receiving His love. This is also why we share Him personally with others. We personally share the Good News with our people because His love is a personal matter.

Does God still personally care about the welfare of the Jewish people? Paul, quoting Isaiah, writes regarding Israel that God's hands are outstretched all day long to a rebellious and disobedient people (Romans 10:21; Isaiah 65:2). He continues to reach out and can't "take the hint." Where are His hands today? They are your hands and my hands. As our hearts are yielded to His heart, our hands reach out on His behalf.

Yeshua wept over Jerusalem because of the lost spiritual state of so many of His people (Luke 19:41). He is still weeping.

But if He weeps and we are unconcerned, then it's not simply the Jewish people with whom we are out of touch. Rather, we are not walking closely with our God, for He personally loves and cares for the lost sheep of the house of Israel.

GOD'S LOVE IS PERPETUAL

When God loves, it is forever. The word "everlasting" in Hebrew is *olam* (which also means "world"). *Olam* comes from the root for secret or hidden. This word gives us a clue as to the unique way that God loves. What we know from experience shows us that everybody has a breaking point and gives up, but the "eternal" by definition is hidden from our experience. In fact, most things of God are beyond human understanding.

This love of God is beyond our understanding. That is why we have "a peace that surpasses comprehension" (Philippians 4:7). I have two sons, and would never give up one of them. But, "God so loved the world He gave His only begotten Son" (John. 3:16). His love for us is based on His character, and His character never changes.

What God declares about Himself is true, and since we are created in His image, we are the objects of His love. Eventually we all mess up. Have others given up on you? Have you given up on others, or yourself? God will never give up on you!

How is God's faithful and perpetual love seen today? Through you, as you continue to pray and reach out to the Jewish people (Romans 10:1). In fact, God has two witnesses to His faithful love today. First, Paul proves that God has not forsaken His people through the witness of Jewish believers that have a present tense Jewish testimony (Romans 11:1-6). In addition, Paul also shows God's faithfulness through the witness of Gentile believers, for they are specifically called to make Israel jealous by ministering His mercy to them (Romans 11:11-31). As His perpetual love in Messiah constrains your heart (2 Corinthians 5:14), you too will reveal His faithful love to Israel.

We will explore the reality that the Body of Messiah must never give up on the Jewish people, because God will never give up on us. His call upon Israel is as sure as His faithfulness to His word. Together we are a living demonstration to the Jewish community of an eternal love that will not give up.

GOD'S LOVE IS POWERFUL

The fact that God loves personally and perpetually is wonderful, and His love also transforms lives. This is because His love is powerful. God continues to draw us to Himself with His lovingkindness, or *chesed* in Hebrew (Jeremiah 31:3). *Chesed* is a word that speaks of a relationship commitment to one another, a covenantal love and kindness. It is what one would expect to receive when in covenant with another, as David said: "Therefore deal kindly with your servant, for you have brought your servant into a covenant of the LORD with you" (1 Samuel 20:8; see also Psalm 89:28).

This helps to explain why Yeshua initially sent His disciples only to the lost sheep of the house of Israel (Matthew 10:5), for they were the inheritors of the Abrahamic covenant with God. Yeshua's reticence in ministering to non-Jews was because they were outside of the Abrahamic Covenant (Matthew 15:26), since all redemptive covenants were made with Israel (Romans 15:8). In Messiah's atonement, non-Jews could accept God's gracious invitation, enter into covenant with God and receive God's *chesed* in Messiah (John 3:16; Ephesians 2:12-13).

How glad I am that it says He will "draw me," not "drive me" to Himself. Though raised in a traditional Jewish home, and become Bar Mitzvah according Orthodox Judaism, I had come to deem all religion as personally irrelevant. Yet the Lord had people risk embarrassment by my sharp tongue to share Messiah with me, invite me to something called a Bible study, and even pray for me—all of which I considered pathetic and silly. I remember mocking the first person who tried to "share the Gospel" with me. Through it all, a spiritual seed was planted in my soul, which was then watered by their prayers as I was spiritually drawn to Messiah. When I came to faith on January 10, 1972, God's love was poured into my heart and I was a new creation in Yeshua. I wrote to that person I had initially mocked several months before, "thank you for letting me laugh at you, for now I love Him, too."

Israel needs to see the Beloved, for many so-called brethren have been mere butchers in the eyes of my people. This love is what is needed for our lives, not merely more rules and regulations. He doesn't draw us with better laws, but with greater love. What's going to bring me all the way to heaven? His love which will never give up or fail me. What will bring national Israel back to God? Israel will be drawn back by God's love—even through you, as you yield your heart and life to Him.

How should I therefore treat others? With better rules and regulations? Relationships work best God's way, through love and mercy. This is how our families, communities, and world are meant to work: in covenant relationship with God and therefore with *chesed* for all. God's great love is going to continue to draw many into His covenant relationship, making us loving instruments of His faithfulness.

For further study:

The reason God called the Jewish people into existence was because He loved them, as He swore over and over again to His people.

> **Deuteronomy 4:37**—Because He loved your fathers, therefore He chose their descendants after them. And He personally brought you from Egypt by His great power.

> **Deuteronomy 10:15**—Yet on your fathers did the LORD set His affection to love them, and He chose their descendants after them, even you above all peoples, as it is this day.

Deuteronomy 23:5—Nevertheless, the LORD your God was not willing to listen to Balaam, but the LORD your God turned the curse into a blessing for you because the LORD your God loves you.

1 Kings 10:9—Blessed be the LORD your God who delighted in you to set you on the throne of Israel; because the LORD loved Israel forever, therefore He made you king, to do justice and righteousness.

2 Chronicles 2:11—Then Huram... answered in a letter sent to Solomon: "Because the LORD loves His people, He has made you king over them."

Isaiah 63:9—In all their affliction He was afflicted, and the angel of His presence saved them; in His love and in His mercy He redeemed them, and He lifted them and carried them all the days of old.

Hosea 3:1—Then the LORD said to me, "Go again, love a woman who is loved by her husband, yet an adulteress, even as the LORD loves the sons of Israel, though they turn to other gods and love raisin cakes."

Hosea 14:4—I will heal their apostasy, I will love them freely, for My anger has turned away from them.

Micah 7:20—You will give truth to Jacob and unchanging love to Abraham, which You swore to our forefathers from the days of old.

GOOD NEWS PRINCIPLES

Tikkun Olam

The Good News is God's way to restore what sin has destroyed. Jewish tradition has a relevant phrase that communicates this idea: *Tikkun Olam*, or "repairing the world." It can connote everything from social justice for orphans to helping the environment. God wants the world restored to His purpose and not merely recreated in our own image.

The triune God created us in His image to rule creation. Now, ruling may suggest domination. But pre-sin, ruling was a responsibility best seen in the command to Adam to cultivate and keep, that is, to serve and protect. In creating Adam in His own image, the Lord then proclaimed that it is not good for man to live alone. We best represent God in loving relationships. We see this relationship re-emphasized by the command that the LORD gave Adam and Eve to "be fruitful and multiply, and fill the earth, and subdue it" (Genesis 1:28). From the beginning, "God blessed *them*," not just him or her. Adam and Eve were blessed in relationship together. They were created with complete dependence on their Creator to fulfill His will.

Our purpose to represent God preceded both sin and salvation. However, with the catastrophic fall in Genesis 3, we need *Tikkun Olam*. The purpose of *Tikkun Olam* is to restore this sin-ruined world; that is, to restore our severed relationship to God and our divided community with each other.

The Good News of Messiah is the realization of the promise to our fathers and God's eternal will for *Tikkun Olam*. Messiah's death and resurrection fulfilled God's original promise. His representatives who value *Tikkun Olam* impact *Olam Hazeh* (this world) through the living witness of *Olam Haba* (the next world) to our people.

2

To the Jew First?

For I am not ashamed of the (Good News,) for it is the power of God for salvation to everyone who believes, to the Jew first and also to the Greek. For in it the righteousness of God is revealed from faith to faith; as it is written, "But the righteous shall live by faith." (Romans 1:16-17)

the good news.

Are we ashamed of the Good News of Messiah? Are you looking for opportunities to share His Message with others, or are you hoping no one will know you are a believer?

Peter denied Messiah three times in shame—"I do not know the man"—yet we have denied Him by omission many more times than Peter. In a great city like Rome, perhaps the congregation was intimidated or ashamed of their fellowship, which was made up mostly of slaves. Some may be ashamed because the Good News seems narrow minded, or "too Gentile." Yet Paul was ready and eager to proclaim the Good News, because he was not ashamed of it.

On the surface the Good News may seem like a ridiculous message: a poor carpenter died for you because you can't save yourself. Yet Paul was unashamed. He was convinced about the testimony of Yeshua and His victory. But that message which so convinced Paul is meaningless if God is not faithful to keeping

His word. This chapter will show how the faithfulness of God necessarily means that the Good News should be "to the Jew first." Then, in the next chapter, we will consider how this unashamed faith has implications not just for "evangelism," but for congregational life as well.

The "Good News" comes from the Hebrew word *besorah* (2 Kings 7:9; Isaiah 40:9). In the Septuagint, or Greek translation of the Hebrew Bible, the word used for *besorah* is *euangelium*, from which we get our English word "evangelism." This has come through the German *gut spiel* to give the English word "gospel." By "Good News," I refer to the apostles' message of the forgiveness of sins:

> Now I make known to you, brethren, the Good News which I preached to you, which also you received, in which also you stand, by which also you are saved, if you hold fast the word which I preached to you, unless you believed in vain. For I delivered to you as of first importance what I also received, that Messiah died for our sins according to the Scriptures, and that He was buried, and that He was raised on the third day according to the Scriptures. (1 Corinthians 15:1-4)

Through Messiah's death and resurrection, we have the message that satisfies the righteous judgment and justice of God; a message which can reconcile and restore every one of us to our Creator. And it's the *only* message of true hope to a decadent and dying world. Outside of the Good News of Messiah, there is no hope.

The Good News is the story of Yeshua, His victory for God, and His power to save. The power was in Yeshua's miraculous virgin birth (Luke 1:35; 2 Peter 1:16). In His life, this power was (and is) for healing (Luke 5:17; 6:19; Mark 6:5). The cross, or death, of Messiah manifests this power for believers, though unbelievers think it is foolishness (1 Corinthians 1:18). Messiah is the power of God for all believers in Yeshua (Ephesians 1:19; 2 Timothy 1:8; 1 Peter 1:5). This power is manifested in believers when we are weak and need to rely on Him (2 Corinthians 4:7; 12:9; 13:4). This power in the *Ruach HaKodesh* (the Holy Spirit) is for our witness (Acts 1:8) and service (Ephesians 3:7; Colossians 1:29). This is resurrection power that will raise us from the dead and transform our mortal flesh into a glorious body (Romans 1:4; 1 Corinthians 6:14; Philippians 3:10).

Though Paul was educated in rabbinics, a scholar of the first rank, bold, and a forceful speaker, his confidence was not because of his own ability (he often admitted to his weakness in this area, 1 Corinthians 2:1-5), but in the Good News itself. God's power in Messiah was enough to fulfill Paul's life forever (Romans 8:37). When considering the eternal power of the Good News, even Rome's great military (the most powerful country of Paul's day) was no comparison. This is the Good News of God's own power in Yeshua —as in Yeshua's birth, life, and resurrection. This power is available to all who rely on Yeshua, to be His witness and live a life pleasing to God. Regardless of the power of sin and pride, God's power is greater!

As a helpless and sinful person, Paul was unashamed, for the Good News has the power. Different views would look to other means of salvation, such as good works:

> R. Joshua b. Levi said: He who joyfully bears the chastisements that befall him brings salvation to the world as it is said, 'Upon them have we stayed of old, that we might be saved' (Ta'anith 8a).

> R. Joshua b. Levi further said: He who calculates his ways in this world will be worthy to behold the salvation of the Holy One, blessed be He (Sotah 5b).

> Even if Israel does before Me but few good deeds at a time, like hens picking in a rubbish heap, I will make it accumulate to a large sum, as it is said, though they pick little they are saved (Avodah Zarah 4a).

According to R. Eleazar: The Lord in His mercy ignores man's sins, so that his good deeds may save him when before the throne of God in judgment (Arachin 8b gloss).

These texts place saving power in man's good works, but the Good News alone is God's power. "I'm unashamed," Paul is saying, "because the Good News alone is the way to God," salvation from the penalty, the power, and ultimately the presence of sin.

Moreover, it is salvation to all who believe. People might think, "Who are you that you think you can personally know the God of creation?" Yet God is no respecter of persons. Through the Jewish Messiah, God was curing a disease that was universal, affecting Jews and Gentiles alike. In God's sight "there are none who do good, no not one" and "all have sinned and fallen short of His glory" (Psalm 14:1; Romans 3:23).

He died for all, but saves all who believe. Anyone who trusts in God's means of salvation will benefit fully and equally. Admittedly, righteousness is not demonstrated perfectly in us, but it is in Him. We must all admit that He alone is worthy and that "there is no good thing in my flesh" (Romans 7:18). His power saves people who are morally marred and spiritually dead. Our weaknesses, not our strengths, actually demonstrate the power of God (2 Corinthians 12:9). Yet He doesn't save those who merely have belief, but those who believe the Good News—those trusting God's way of salvation in Yeshua. It is not faith that saves you, but faith in Yeshua, the salvation God has provided in Him that saves you when you believe.

Therefore, those who might say that God saves all sincere, religious Jews who do not believe in Yeshua are sadly mistaken. God will save all who believe in Messiah Yeshua, but not unless they believe. Paul, a rabbi who came to personal faith in Yeshua, refers to Jewish people who strive to keep the Mosaic *torah* when he says that they "pursued a law of righteousness, but did not arrive at that law… they have a zeal for God but not according to knowledge… they attempted to establish their own righteousness not knowing about God's righteousness." Paul understood that, "Messiah is the goal of *torah* for righteousness to all who believe" (Romans 9:31-10:4).

Jews who have not trusted in Messiah Yeshua are still lost and need to be saved. The salvation of national Israel is Paul's "heart's desire and prayer to God" (Romans 10:1). Contrary to the opinions of some, there is no unrecognized mediation of Yeshua that saves any religious people, Jew or Gentile, who have not personally trusted in Messiah Yeshua. Faith in Yeshua actually demonstrates genuine saving faith in God (2 John 9). The amount of faith you have is not at issue, but the object of your faith is. The salvation which God has provided in the Messiah is what saves you. His righteousness is revealed in the Good News (Romans 1:17) by faith based on His righteousness, not your own deeds!

Thus, although Paul had nothing in his flesh in which he could boast, he was unashamed, for the Good News is salvation for all by faith in Messiah Yeshua.

But though this Good News is to all who believe, Paul writes that it is to the Jew first, and also to the Greek. It is to this phrase we now turn.

WHAT DOES "TO THE JEW FIRST" MEAN?

A common idea is that "to the Jew first" means "first the Good News went to the Jews, and now it is going to the Gentile." One might call this the *historical* interpretation. This seems to make sense, because after all, as a matter of historical order, Gentiles received the Good News *after* the Jewish people. The New International Version (NIV) leaves open this interpretation when it translates the Greek: "first for the Jew, then for the Gentile" (inserting "then"). Now, if this historical interpretation is true, then it is hard to imagine the idea having much ongoing significance today. "To the Jew first" may have to be viewed as an interesting cultural artifact, like the commands for a woman to cover her head, but believers would not be wise to treat it as a foundational value.

For comparison, consider how David Stern, in his *Complete Jewish Bible*, translates this phrase of Romans 1:16, "to the Jew especially, but equally to the Gentile." The Good News is offered "equally" to Gentiles; thus, it is "also" for the Gentiles (NASB). By faith in Yeshua, anyone, regardless of ethnicity, may be "delivered from the domain of darkness unto the kingdom of His beloved Son" (Colossians 1:13). However, in this viewpoint, while the Good News is equally for Gentiles, it is *especially* for the Jewish people. In this reading, Paul was not trying to simply convey what happened historically, but make a point of deeper significance about the Good News.

Which reading is correct? We must determine the best reading not merely to know which translation to choose, but in order to understand and apply God's Word. There are three reasons to reject the historical interpretation.

First, it is grammatically incorrect because of the meaning of the adjective "first." The word for "first" in Romans 1:16 is *proton*. Michael Rydelnik, Professor of Jewish Studies at Moody Bible Institute points out if Paul had meant "formerly" or "earlier," he would have used a different Greek word: *proteron*. The same word *proton* is also used in Romans 2:9-10 and 3:2.

> Tribulation and distress for every soul of man who does evil, of the Jew first (*proton*) and also of the Greek. But glory and honor and peace to everyone who does good, to the Jew first (*proton*) and also to the Greek. (Romans 2:9-10)

> First of all (*proton*), that they were entrusted with the oracles of God. (Romans 3:2)

This same phrase "First of all," in the New American Standard (NASB), and "in the first place" in the New Revised

Standard (NRSV), is translated by the New King James version as "chiefly."

Second, it is grammatically incorrect because of the verbs: the whole verse is in the present tense. Three Greek verbs are found in Romans 1:16: "am unashamed," "is," and "believes." All three are present tense. So the phrase "to the Jew first" should be understood in the present tense as well. The phrase would need a different modifying verb form if the author wanted to say it *was* to the Jew first.

In other words, if we allow the phrase to imply it is no longer presently "to the Jew first," then we have to be consistent: it is no longer "to all who will believe," no longer "the power of God for salvation." And so perhaps we need to be more "ashamed" of our faith in Yeshua and not be so eager to share Him. That is simply folly.

Third, the idea of "first" reiterates the Jewish people's chosen priority, and this is not limited to a sequential order of receiving the Good News. Peter concluded his preaching to the "men of Israel" (Acts 3:12-26), by saying:

> You are the sons of the prophets and of the covenant that God made with your fathers, saying to Abraham, "And in your offspring shall all the families of the earth be blessed." God, having raised up His Servant, sent Him to you first, to bless you by turning every one of you from your evil ways. (Acts 3:25-26)

Peter had not yet received the vision showing how the Good News would go to the Gentiles (Acts 10). At that time the Good News was only going to the Jewish people, from the past until the present. In Romans, Paul is reinforcing "to the Jew first" in this sense of priority which Peter lays out.

Just as God declared, the Jewish people are His "chosen people" (Deuteronomy 7:6). There is no case for Jewish pride here, because the Scriptures explain:

> The LORD did not set His love on you nor choose you because you were more in number than any of the peoples, for you were the fewest of all peoples, but because the LORD loved you and kept the oath which He swore to your forefathers, the LORD brought you out by a mighty hand and redeemed you from the house of slavery, from the hand of Pharaoh king of Egypt. (Deuteronomy 7:8-9; cf. 9:6)

I understand how one might feel uncomfortable with this notion of chosenness, thinking that it reflects a sense of innate superiority. Others may think it right to obsess over or show favoritism to the Jewish people in their chosen position.

However, if we simply accept the biblical premise, we see that Jewish people were not chosen to exhibit their own spirituality, but to demonstrate the ability of God. Thus, the Good News is the power of God manifested. If a lion tamer wanted to prove his greatness as a tamer of lions, would he choose a lion any child could tame, or the most unmanageable lion? The issue of "to the Jew first" is meant to focus us upon God's faithfulness, not ours, for it is He Who did "not forsake a people Whom He foreknew" (Romans 11:1-2).

God has no "plan B"—for example, "in case of national Jewish rejection of Messiah, replace with Gentiles." Rather, Yeshua is God's faithfulness to His plan. It is because of His plan, which is to the Jew first, that the promises are confirmed and made available to all who will believe (Romans 15:9).

WHAT TRANSLATION REFLECTS ACTUAL HISTORY?

In regards to the general work of the Good News, the idea that the Good News was "first for the Jew and then for the Gentile" implies that the Good News is no longer going to the Jew. Some argue that when Paul became frustrated with the Jewish people's unwillingness to believe in Yeshua he therefore "turned to the Gentiles" (Acts 13:46).

While it is true that the Gentiles received the Good News after the Jews, that's not the whole picture. In fact, in that same verse, he says, "It was necessary that the Good News be brought first to the Jewish people." Why was it necessary? Paul understood that the Good News was always to the Jew first, because God in Messiah had not "forsaken the Jewish people" (Romans 11:1). Thus, in the next town, Paul immediately went to the Jewish people with the Good News (Acts 14:1). The Good News continued to go to the Jewish people first even after going to the Gentiles.

Paul was writing "to the Jew first," not regarding a past activity, but as his present ministry (Acts 13:46; 14:1; Romans 9:1-4). Though it is true that the Good News spread to the Gentiles after the Jewish people in the first century, Paul was communicating a different point. "To the Jew first" was an ongoing principle for Paul in the flow of history, and his own service. We have to interpret it from where he was standing. He was not "looking back" on the first century advance of the Good News, as some interpreters might today, but stating it as an ongoing principle for the present and future flow of history.

As an apostle to the Gentiles (Romans 11:13), his present ministry was "to the Jew first." This was exactly what he wanted this Roman congregation to understand about the basic issues of the Good News. It is and always will be the power of God unto salvation, for all who believe, and to the Jew first.

The danger of mistranslating and misunderstanding "to the Jew first" implies that the Good News no longer has to go to the Jews, that God's promises to the Jewish people are voided, or that those promises transferred to the Church. These ideas suggest that "God has forsaken the Jewish people." This is impossible! How then could anyone trust in any of God's promises, if His promises to Israel are nullified? Paul's point was not to undermine their confidence in Messiah, but to establish their confidence in the Good News.

THE KEY THAT UNLOCKS THE BOOK

The Good News of Messiah fulfills the promises that God made to the Jewish people to redeem them and the Nations (Genesis 12:3). Most conservative scholars agree that Romans 1:16-17 are the theme for the book of Romans; that is, they are the key to understanding the rest of the book. For most believers, the book of Romans provides the essence of New Covenant teaching. Likewise, followers of Yeshua understand that the New Covenant gives the outworking or fulfillment of the very message of the *Tanakh*. Thus, these verses provide us with a theme to understand not only the book itself, but the whole of Scripture!

Since God is faithful to His word, "to the Jew first" recognizes the unchanged reality of the Jewish people. The whole book is to be understood in Jewish terms. Romans, a book for all Gentiles from the Apostle to the Gentiles, has a "to the Jew first" message.

- ✡ It is a fulfillment of the promises made in the prophets (Romans 1:2).
- ✡ Yeshua is David's Son according to the flesh (Romans 1:3), and is introduced to the Nations by a redeemed Israelite (Romans 11:1, 13).
- ✡ "To the Jew first" is reiterated as principle regarding reward and judgment (Romans 2:9-10).
- ✡ Salvation by faith in Messiah is "to the Jew first" as understood through the teaching of the *Tanakh* and the examples of Abraham and Adam (Romans 1:17; 4; 5:12-21).

Paul wanted the Gentiles to know of their responsibility to understand and express their faith in light of God's faithfulness to Israel. "To the Jew first" for the Gentile believers was a reminder of their calling to make Israel jealous, and to minister the mercy they had received (Romans 11:11, 31). God forbid that Gentiles should think that they had replaced Israel! No, rather Gentile believers were to be God's reminders of His faithfulness *to* Israel. Any Gentile who would not go "to the Jew first" would be distorting God's message of faithfulness in the Good News, in that he would attempt to cancel God's promise.

We are obligated, eager, and unashamed of the Good News, because we are unashamed of His power, righteousness, faithfulness, and eternal dependability. "To the Jew first" should be the motto of all believers throughout this age as they depend upon and proclaim the Good News of Messiah.

The Good News is always "to the Jew first" because God never made a covenantal promise of redemption with any people other than the Jewish people. The covenantal promise with Abraham and his seed is the only hope of the nations, including the Jewish people. God would never righteously save anyone apart from what He promised Israel.

KEEP IT FUNCTIONAL

Single-cell bacteria propel themselves a whip-like tail connected to an outboard motor, called a "flagellum." Top engineers study its construction and speed capabilities, with the hopes that its secrets can be applied to their own lesser nanotechnology. Biochemist Michael Behe used a term "irreducible complexity" to try to describe this wonder, among other things, like the eye and blood clotting. Irreducible complexity means that all its parts are arranged in careful dependence upon the others. Without any given part, the machine as a whole will not function.

No one would have imagined even a century ago what was happening all along, in just a tiny cell! But the way in which the God of Israel demonstrates His righteousness in Messiah is similar to the way He has created these brilliant biological machines. His covenantal promises are complex, and they cannot be reduced by any one part.

The Abrahamic covenant promised blessing for the nations—that is, all the Gentiles—in Abraham's seed. Yet this same covenant also promised Abraham a people and a land. It is one, irreducibly complex covenant. If God were to fulfill one part of the promise but nullify another part, He would break the covenant, which would be unrighteous to Abraham and his descendants. It would be dead, cancelled. If the land is no longer for them, then they need no longer be a people, and no longer any promise in blessing to all nations in his seed, Messiah. That's true by design.

Similarly, this three-fold Good News that reveals God's righteousness in Messiah is also irreducibly complex. All the pieces matter—if indeed "therein is the righteousness of God." If we take away even a part—whether it be that the Good News is "the power of God," "to every one that believes," or "to the Jew first"—then we make the righteousness of God into unrighteousness. The only hope for the Gentile world is that the Good News of Messiah is to the Jew first.

Without His power unto salvation in Yeshua, God is not saving anyone. Without His salvation received by faith in Yeshua—"to all who believe"—there would be no salvation for Jews or Gentiles, since all have free will. And apart from the Good News being to the Jew first and equally to the Gentile, God is unfaithful to His own promises and is untrustworthy for any to believe. If we remove any element then we have a different message that defames God's righteous character; one element cannot be removed without annulling the very function of the Good News.

God's righteousness is revealed in the Good News. The Good News is both a demonstration of God's power and a revelation of God's righteousness. This is exactly what Paul stated in Romans 1:17 to explain why he is unashamed of the Good News: "For in it the righteousness of God is revealed… just as it is written." God's righteousness is revealed through His desire to save sinners and not judge them. It is a righteous salvation because it's by faith and to the Jew first. In other words, if it was not to the Jew first, it would not reveal His righteousness as being faithful to His word. The fulfillment of His promises is not merely seen in the various prophecies predicting Messiah, but also in the context of Yeshua being the Redeemer of Israel. What is understood as a prophecy of His rejection by Israel in Isaiah 53 is actually a prophecy that Israel will repent and trust in Messiah Yeshua.

Paul was unashamed because the Good News is the faithfulness of God to our people. The Good News is still to the Jew first, even as it is still the power of God unto salvation to all who will believe! God is faithful, and all who believe on His promised salvation in Yeshua will indeed be saved.

There is a story of a Nazi that needed a heart transplant in order to live. The doctor rushed in to tell him that a man who just passed away was the only available donor—but the man was a Jew! The Nazi thought, "I want to live, but do I want to live bad enough to live with a Jewish heart?" God wants you to live eternally with the King of the Jews in your life—but in order to truly live, you'll live with His Jewish heart, and the love of Messiah will constrain your own heart. There is no disgrace trusting in His grace.

GOOD NEWS PRINCIPLES

Kiddush HaShem

How does the Good News connect with God's holiness? Here we must consider a foundational biblical concept called *Kiddush HaShem*, or Sanctification of the Name. God's "Name" doesn't just mean a given name like "Sam," but it speaks of His character or reputation. Since we were created in God's image, when we sinned we brought desecration to His name. But God's reputation, his righteous character, must and will remain holy, or set apart.

> *You shall not profane My holy name, but I will be sanctified among the sons of Israel; I am the LORD who sanctifies you. (Leviticus 22:32)*

Messiah lived and died for *Kiddush HaShem*, the sanctification of the Name. Even as the ultimate desecration of the Name is our sinfulness, so also the ultimate sanctification of the Name is Yeshua's sacrifice for our sins.

In traditional Judaism, a righteous martyr makes *Kiddush HaShem* when he willingly gives up his life rather than commit a grave sin against God's name. For example, according to tradition Rabbi Akiba sanctified the Name in 132 AD when, being tortured to death by the Romans, he refused idolatry and died with the confession of the One God on his lips. However, the Lord Yeshua went further. Not only did He die rather than tarnish God's name by any sinful action, but He died so as to reverse and remove our desecration of HaShem!

The Good News is only validated as God's righteousness is revealed. Paul's theme in Romans is that the Good News of Yeshua reveals God's righteousness, in other words, sanctifies God's Name.

> *Our Father in heaven, may your Name be sanctified! (Matthew 6:9)*

3

The Necessity of Messianic Congregations

We have considered the Good News priority toward the Jewish people. Now in this chapter we will consider the implications for congregational life.

The existence of Messianic congregations testifies to God's triumph. However, not everyone knows a triumph when they see one! Years ago, there was a church in New York City that graciously allowed me to use their building for a monthly outreach to Jewish people. On one occasion when I called to schedule the date for the upcoming month, the pastor explained with excitement that the space wouldn't be available. "We're having evangelistic training," the pastor explained. "We're going to have everyone witnessing, and we'll need the space for all the new believers."

A month later I received a call from the pastor, now somewhat disheartened. "You can use any space in the building you want. Though we had the whole congregation witnessing, no one was saved! Our evangelistic efforts were a total failure!"

"Pastor, you're completely wrong," I replied, taken aback by his comment. "It was a great success—if you had everyone in your congregation witnessing, that's a great victory!" Because of inadequate evaluation, we might not know a success when we have one!

A MESSIANIC CONGREGATION IS THE FAITHFUL TESTIMONY OF GOD

It is my desire and goal for "all Israel to be saved," that is, for the Jewish people as a whole to come to personal faith in Messiah Yeshua (Romans 10:1; 11:26). Unfortunately there is a problem with this lofty goal. The Jewish believer has a dilemma of faithfulness. Think about this: What if every Jewish person came to faith in Messiah and was saved—where would they go to fellowship and grow in the faith? For even if they went to whatever might be considered a "good church" (doctrinally sound with a pro-Israel stance, etc.), within two generations, would there be any Jewish identity left?

In Jeremiah 31:35-37 God has made a gracious commitment to preserve the Jewish people as an identifiable nation:

> Thus says the LORD, Who gives the sun for light by day, and the fixed order of the moon and the stars for light by night, Who stirs up the sea so that its waves roar; The LORD of hosts is His name; "If this fixed order departs from before Me," declares the LORD, "then the offspring of Israel also will cease from being a nation forever." Thus says the LORD, "If the heavens above can be measured and the foundations of the earth searched out below, then I will also cast off all the offspring of Israel for all that they have done," declares the LORD.

God's word declares that my people will continue to exist, and the created order is His guarantee. By keeping Israel according to His promises God shows that He can keep all people. However, if all Jewish people were saved and assimilated into good churches, as such churches exist today, the Jewish people as a nation would virtually end.

The congregational culture and discipleship of even the best churches remains insufficient for Jewish believers to not only retain their Jewish identity but pass on their Jewish heritage to their children. Traditional Christendom is steeped in assumptions which suppress Jewish continuity. Because of tradition, even the best churches are not established in such a way to include Jewish believers as Jews. Without this inclusion, what remains is a vague sense of Jewish presence, disregarded as irrelevant and curious on the one hand, and regarded with a mix of fetish and disdain on the other.

I have met many Jewish children of believers growing up outside the Messianic community. Sadly, in general, they have at best a vague sense of their own Jewishness, and tend not to see its relevance. People tell me so often, "I think my grandpa was Jewish." A worse attitude can result where one's Jewish identity was over-emphasized, being looked at as a unparalleled source for the "Jewish perspective" on the Scriptures, as though a Jewish believer is meant to live up to the Christian stereotype.

Either attitude towards Jewish identity will mean the death of the Jewish community. If Yeshua is actually the Jewish Messiah, then it is in Him that my people truly live as a people, rather than forget who we are. And if Yeshua is the Jewish Messiah, then it is anti-Semitic and against the promises of God to suggest that this preservation ought to happen apart from trust in Him and participation in His body.

Perhaps surprisingly, the Messianic congregation is also the place for Gentiles to demonstrate God's faithfulness. We will go into that matter in more depth when we consider the calling that God has on every Gentile believer. However, for the sake of God's promises, let it be stressed that we want the Jewish people to endure in Messiah, and do so without unbiblical dysfunctions. His faithfulness is on the line.

A MESSIANIC CONGREGATION IS THE EFFECTIVE TESTIMONY OF GOD

By "effective," I don't mean more decisions or "converts" for Messiah, but rather a clearer and more direct communication of the Good News. A Messianic congregation is not only God's gracious commitment but also good communication of His love and grace in Messiah. A man named Rich Freeman had many objections to faith in Messiah Yeshua. Primarily, since he was Jewish, he was sure that faith in Jesus was not for him. However, when he entered a Messianic congregation for the first time, all his excuses vanished in the reality of Jewish worship in Yeshua's name. In that service he heard and understood the message of Messiah, His death for our sins, and the need to believe on Him for salvation. Rich trusted in Messiah and is now following the Lord and serving in Messianic Jewish ministry as well.

It is true that Messianic congregational ministry, or Jewish ministry in general, is often not seen as much of a success. In a world of megachurches, this is micro-ministry. Perhaps a couple military examples can put it in perspective. General George Patton led the US Third Army during World War II. He marched from France to Germany and utterly destroyed their armed forces, winning so quickly and decisively that his position could not be kept on the map!

Now consider the 1967 battle for Jerusalem. It cost the Israeli Defense Forces so much in human losses in order to gain just another doorway, just another square foot of that city.

You might say that in comparison with Patton's European victory, Jerusalem wasn't worth the effort. Yet the value was not found in size, but strategy. Likewise, the Scriptures teach us to say, "If I forget you O Jerusalem, may my right hand lose its cunning" (Psalm 137:5).

Jewish ministry could seem to cost too much for too little gain. Yet, in God's sight, it is worth every sacrifice. Why? It is worth it because the Messianic congregation is the most effective expression of the Good News to the Jewish people and all people—precisely because it effectively communicates the faithfulness of God, that He has not forsaken a people whom He foreknew (Romans 11:1-2). Though Jews and Gentiles are equal in Messiah, the truth is that Jews remain Jews without any trace of sinful pride, while Gentiles remain Gentiles without any sense of inequality. This presents the fulfillment of the Abrahamic Covenant in Messiah Yeshua—Jewish and Gentile believers honoring Yeshua as Lord in unity and love.

The concern of the Jewish community is not the prophecy of Isaiah 53 (though I wish it was as it will be one day); rather, the issue concerning the Jewish community is community —will the Jewish people continue as a people? A Messianic congregation is a community, therefore it effectively answers the how's and why's of Jewish community.

From the beginning, God's testimony was to be an assembly, a community of believers—not one or two Jews who happen to believe in some non-Jewish matter. Though God had in Abraham one suitable believer, He said He would make of Him "a nation" (Genesis 12:2). It would be the continuing community that would evidence the faithfulness of Abraham's God. Similarly, Yeshua said to Peter and company, "On this Rock, I will build my assembly" (Matthew 16:18). Thus, an ongoing community must be what testifies *Am Yisrael chai b'Shem Yeshua*, "the people of Israel live, in the name of Yeshua!"

This concern is not just that of the traditional Jewish community, but as Jeremiah 31:35-37 shows, it is also God's concern! Therefore, this should be every believer's concern, whether Jewish or Gentile. The endurance of the Jewish people should be foundational for how we conceive of our corporate testimony in Messiah.

Effectiveness in communication is seen in how well the Good News is understood. Some Christian leaders have accused Messianic congregations of "diluting the biblical message" with Jewish ideas and symbols as a means of "luring ignorant Jews into Christianity." My response to them was, "so in expressing your faith, are you using your Gentile culture to lure in ignorant Gentiles?" Of course not, but since many identify their faith by their culture, they think that a change in cultural expression is a change in the actual faith as well. On the contrary, by expressing our faith through its biblically Jewish orientation, the witness to the Jewish community is more faithful. How? A Messianic congregation communicates the Good News in such a clear way that Jewish people cannot help but get the message, that to believe in the Jewish Messiah is the most Jewish thing any Jew could do.

This effectiveness is not to be confused with expediency. An effective testimony will sometimes draw a reaction before you get a response. In fact, if the message is undiluted and thus more clearly portrayed, it may be seen as more threatening by the Jewish establishment. In fact, Yeshua demonstrated that if you are perfectly effective, it may get you crucified! Yet, you cannot be effective if you're not communicating the Good News in a way people can understand it. This is what Paul taught:

> For if I preach the gospel, I have nothing to boast of, for I am under compulsion; for woe is me if I do not preach the Good News... For though I am free from all men, I have made myself a slave to all, so that I may win more. To the Jews I became as a Jew, so that I might win Jews; to those who are under the Law, as under the Law though not being myself under the Law, so that I might win those who are under the Law. (1 Corinthians 9:19-20)

God forbid that he not preach the Good News—this is faithfulness. He preached it unto the Jews as a Jew, to those under the Law as under the Law, so that some might be saved—and this is effectiveness.

A MESSIANIC CONGREGATION IS THE FULFILLING TESTIMONY OF GOD

A Messianic congregation is not only God's gracious commitment, not only His good communication, but it is essential in His Great Commission (Matthew 28:18-20).

Yeshua has "all the authority in heaven and on earth," and with that authority He has commanded us to make disciples (Matthew 28:18). If we are convinced of His Lordship, we must therefore be committed to His discipleship, for He said, "Go, therefore and make disciples of all nations" (Matthew 28:19). This means raising new believers in the faith so that they will live out God's faithfulness in their circumstances.

It starts with immersion, which testifies publicly to what the Spirit did at salvation: identifying the new believer with the Lord (Matthew 28:20). However, discipleship is not only the one time act, but it is the ongoing activity of growing as believers in all that Yeshua has commanded. We are to teach the truth, not merely transfer information, so that believers will observe, or do, all that Yeshua commanded.

The primary function of any congregation is as a disciple-making center, even as the Lord's faithfulness is fully seen in a discipled believer. Remember the minister in NY who thought his congregation's outreach efforts were a total failure because no one was "saved"? What this evaluation failed to consider was that the habit of having his congregants sharing their faith should be a part of their healthy growth as disciples. It is healthy disciples, not larger numbers, which is the goal of the congregation.

What does this have to do with a Messianic congregation? Well, the undiscipled believer is an unfaithful believer. Our faithfulness is to demonstrate the faithfulness of God in Messiah, since we are to reflect Him (1 Peter 1:15; Leviticus 19:2). Just as God is committed to keep the Jewish people as a people, so every believer is to have this same commitment.

When the child of a Jewish believer does not say, "I am a Jew" (Acts 22:3), but instead proclaims through his words or actions, "I think my dad or mom was Jewish," this does not just reflect a poor testimony of the body of Messiah, but also reflects poor discipleship. This in turn only gives Messiah a bad name in the Jewish community, but the real failure was the breach in following Yeshua.

If a new believer understands his or her Jewish identity in Messiah, then this same God who promised that He would not "leave nor forsake our people" is seen in the eyes of the Jewish community, and to all who are looking, as the same faithful Lord who said, "I am with you always to the end of the age" (Joshua 1:9; Matthew 28:20). Also, as Gentiles are saved through the evangelistic work of Messianic congregations ("also to the Gentile," right?), they will be grounded and grow in the same faith, by the same discipleship. This makes their own communication of the Good News more clear and meaningful to the Jewish people and all people.

Thus, there must be Messianic congregations, for the faithfulness of God must be lived out by the body of Messiah. When Yeshua's faithfulness is demonstrated in His followers, then His fellowship with us is seen through Messianic communities (Matthew 18:20). As we are convinced of His Lordship, and therefore committed to His discipleship, we also demonstrate that we are complete in His fellowship. Messianic congregations are the living testimonies of God's triumph in Messiah. They reveal God's faithfulness in Messiah Yeshua to eyes that see, ears that hear, and hearts that desire after Him.

GOOD NEWS PRINCIPLES

Am Yisrael Chai

Often our heart concern for the Jewish people is, understandably, that individuals would see Yeshua through the prophets, like Isaiah 53. Yet, the more immediate Jewish concern has been to survive and thrive as a people—a value which is often summed up in the phrase *Am Yisrael Chai* (the people of Israel live).

The body of Messiah in general, and the Messianic congregation in particular, are established by God to represent to the world His faithfulness in Messiah, to "keep a people whom He foreknew" (Romans 11:2). Congregations are called both to share in and speak to this divine concern, thus testifying of Messiah's faithfulness to Israel. Believing communities identify with Israel.

The importance of the Jewish community's visible existence is God's faithfulness to His word. God started with one man, and said, "I will make of you a people" (Genesis 12:2). With Abraham and Sarah who were unable to naturally have a child, He produced a people as proof of His faithfulness and power. God's testimony of faithfulness to His promise is seen in a community of Jewish people, not just in the individual Jewish believer. Therefore Yeshua said that "upon this rock" He would build a community that testifies of His faithfulness.

The credential that the Jewish Messiah has a sovereign impact on the nations for Israel's good is vital to the Hebrew Scriptures and the rabbinical writings. The congregation's testimony pictures a restored Israel with the Nations in the commonwealth of Israel (Genesis 35:11; Ephesians 2:12-13). So also, the congregation is the Jewish olive tree through which both present tense Jews and Gentiles proclaim the Good News that in Messiah: God is faithful to Israel. May the people of Israel live in Yeshua the Messiah!

Listen to me, you who pursue righteousness, who seek the Lord, look to the rock from which you were hewn, and to the quarry from which you were dug.

Isaiah 51:1

4

The Faith of Our Fathers

How can we have assurance of being right with God? We are sinners. We have so much fear, disappointment, and bitterness. How can we know that God hasn't forsaken us? Does He really accept us as we are? Once after Shabbat classes an 11-year-old boy was asked by his mom what he had learned that morning. "Well," Josh said, "our teacher told us how God sent Moses behind enemy lines to rescue the Israelis from the Egyptians. Moses led them to the Red Sea and then ordered his engineers to build a bridge. After they all crossed, they saw the Egyptian tanks coming, so Moses radioed the Israeli Air Force and they sent jet fighters, who bombed the bridge and saved the Jews." Josh's mother looked at him sideways and said, "Josh, is that really the way that your teacher told the story?"

"Not really," Josh admitted. "But if I told it her way, you'd *never* believe it."

Regarding salvation, Yeshua Himself explained to His own mystified disciples, "With men this is impossible, but with God all things are possible" (Matthew 19:26). So it was with Abraham. Though Abraham believed God, he was confused about God's promise of a seed, so he cried out to God and told Him that his only heir was his servant, Eliezer (Genesis 15).

In the midst of this narrative we find a profound theological statement regarding Abraham: "and he believed the LORD; and He reckoned it to him as righteousness" (Genesis 15:6). If Abraham was struggling, then it seems that having struggles with God is not a sign of unbelief. Yet, what about the fear and disappointment? How can we be sure that God is with us and has a plan for us? How can we have assurance of being right with God? Is it through heroic *torah*-obedience? No, but if I told you what the Scripture does say, you might never believe it! The assurance that we are made right with God is the same assurance that Abraham had. To understand the role of faith in God's calling for Messianic Jews, we will consider three things about how Abraham believed God:

- ✡ His faith was personal. He did not merely believe about God, but in Him.
- ✡ His faith was propositional. Believing in the person of God meant faith in the promises of God.
- ✡ His faith was practical. Belief necessitated action.

FAITH IS RELIANCE UPON GOD'S PROMISES

Abraham had faith in God. His genuine faith was seen in his responses to God's promises. This idea is highlighted in the text with the first word "and" (the letter *vav* in Hebrew) at the beginning of the verse. This conjunction "and" ties it to the previous verse, where God directed Abraham to look to the night sky and said, "So shall your seed be" (Genesis 15:5).

Faith is a response to God's promise, not our own imagination of what we want. Abraham's life of faith is seen in three periods of growth in Genesis:

- ✡ The period of his calling, Genesis 12-14
- ✡ The period of his covenants, Genesis 15-21
- ✡ The period of his confirmation, Genesis 22-25

In the New Covenant, we are informed in Genesis 12 that Abraham had been saved by faith when he first believed: "By faith Abraham, when he was called, obeyed by going out" (Hebrews 11:8). The primary salvation truth found in Genesis 15:6 marks each of the three periods of Abraham's life, and it is used in the New Covenant to characterize each period in His faith development (Romans 4:3; Galatians 3:6; Jacob 2:23).

Stage 1: Salvation Commences By Faith

Romans 4 is Paul's commentary or *midrash* on Genesis 15:6 that portrays Abraham as the father of faith. The text in Romans states that *he believed* the Lord:

He believed the Lord for many descendants (Genesis 15:5). What if Abraham prayed something like this: "That's nice, God, but I'd like just two kids, a boy and a girl, healthy, intelligent, good looking, athletic, with good careers, and a few grandkids. Thanks." Of course he then added, "And I really believe you can do it!" What would be the result of such belief? It would not be reckoned as righteousness, unlike faith in God's Word.

He believed the Lord for one Glorious Descendent. The word "seed" in Genesis 15 is in the singular because it was pointing to Messiah. As Yeshua observed, "Abraham was glad to see My day, and he did see it" (John 8:58). For within the promises made to Abraham was the essential truth that Messiah was the goal of them all, even as Adam was assured in Genesis 3:15. Indeed, Yeshua is the very righteousness to which all *torah* (Law) would witness (Romans 3:21; 10:4). The demons believe God and tremble, but we believe in God and trust.

He believed the Lord apart from any natural means and that all would be accomplished through the power of God. Faith is trusting God despite the circumstances. It is not weakened or diminished by them. Faith trusts God's power without denying our inability or wavering with inner disputes over the immensity of the promise. Abraham never denied his own inability, but trusted in what he believed God could do! Rather, he was strengthened in faith, as he gave glory to God, and he was confident and fully persuaded in the character of God as well as His power. This faith was credited to him as righteousness (Romans 4:22).

Like Abraham, we are to contemplate that our bodies are as good as dead because of sin. As Abraham believed that the God who created the stars could create seed and life from him and Sarah, so also we are to believe that this God who created life was able to raise Yeshua from the dead (Romans 4:23-25). The whole Scriptures assure us that we are relating to God only when we are relying on His promises.

Stage 2: Salvation Continues By Faith

Faith relies upon the promises: "Abraham believed" (Genesis 15:6). The word "believed" in Hebrew is *he'emin*, whose root means sure, stable, certain, fixed, or firm. Another word we get from this root, *amen*, concludes many prayers; it does not proclaim "may it be so," but that it is so! Faith does not believe that God can, but that He will.

Why does salvation continue in faith? God's power in your life is manifested only in the context of relationship. A relationship with God, like all other healthy relationships, is based on trust. In Galatians 3:1-5, Paul was amazed that the Gentile Galatians who began by faith were spiritually 'changing horses in mid-stream', attempting to rely on their works to obtain God's blessings. He writes:

> Even so Abraham believed God, and it was credited to him as righteousness. Therefore, be sure that it is those who are of faith who are sons of Abraham. The Scripture, foreseeing that God would justify the Gentiles by faith, preached the gospel beforehand to Abraham, saying, "All nations will be blessed through you." So then those who are of faith are blessed with Abraham, the believer. (Galatians 3:6-9)

In 3:6, Paul repeats the Genesis 15:6 promise as to how Abraham continued in faith. Salvation both starts and continues by faith not works, because God's blessing flows from His justifying us by faith in Yeshua. Just as Messiah had been "portrayed" (3:1) or "placarded" before the Galatians, so also the promise had been "placarded" before Abraham in the stars.

Like Abraham, the father of faith, we continue by faith in his promises not by works of our own efforts. The phrase, "he believed," is in the perfect tense: believed and continued to believe. Marriage vows are not merely that "I do (today)," but "I do and I will (always)." Salvation begins and continues by faith. Covenant merely formalizes and clarifies that faith relationship. Ceremonies such as the covenant of circumcision or *brit milah* signify and testify to the faith relationship. Paul explains this in Romans 4:11-12:

> And he received the sign of circumcision, a seal of the righteousness of the faith which he had while uncircumcised, so that he might be the father of all who believe without being circumcised, that righteousness might be credited to them, and the father of circumcision to those who not only are of the circumcision, but who also follow in the steps of the faith of our father Abraham which he had while uncircumcised.

Some might say, "I want Him to speak to me too, and then I will believe." However, then you will merely believe your experience, not His Word. The Bible is His Word, and we are to depend on His Word, not our experience. Yeshua teaches that if people do not believe God's Word, then they will not believe even if someone is raised from the dead (Luke 16:31). It is not your faith in your experience that saves you, but your faith in God and in His Word. Abraham depending on his experiences thought that Eliezer would be his heir. However, God's Word contradicted his experience. God develops our faith to turn from our plans to His promises.

Stage 3: Salvation Is Perfected By Faith

For Abraham, faith was seen in his reverence for the Promise Keeper. The text says that he believed "in the Lord" (Jacob or "James" 2:23). Abraham's faith was focused not in the *promises*, but in the One who made them. Faith is only as effective as the object of faith. God as the Promise Maker is worthy of your trust as the Promise Keeper.

It is faith in the fulfillment of His promises that has us respond with faithfulness and obedience. This aspect of faith brings change, transformation, and completion. Faith flowers into works. As faith is the simple reliance upon God's ability to do as He has promised, that same faith blooms into wholehearted obedience in believers doing as He commanded. Reliance is not just mental assent. Though we are saved purely by grace through faith and not by our good works, we are surely saved in order to do good works (Ephesians 2:8-10). In the New Covenant, Paul called this the "obedience of faith" or "faith obedience" (Romans 1:5; 16:26). Salvation anticipates transformation. Faith is the essence of all true righteousness, which is consistently evidenced through proper actions toward God and man.

Righteousness intrinsically contains trust in God that reveals His concern for others through all our actions. Thus all faith in God is a reliance on His great concern for humanity that shows itself in His fulfillment of His promises.

To the degree that you have reliance, to that degree you have obedience. Growth is not a matter of forcing more works out, but of developing faith and reliance upon God. The more you understand His faithfulness, the more you can trust in Him. And the more you trust in Him, the more you will desire to follow Him, do His will, live out His love and life, and be thereby transformed into His likeness. As you develop unquestioning reliance, you respond to God with unquestioning obedience. This is the perfecting of your faith.

Abraham's faith, as demonstrated in the offering of Isaac, is said to be perfected by works, indeed it says he was justified by works (Jacob 2:23). Well the word "justified" is better translated "vindicated" as in 1 Timothy 3:16. Thus faith is reckoned as righteousness, not as a substitute for doing what is right, but as the foundation for transformation. In Abraham's works of offering Isaac in Genesis 22:16-18, the declaration that his deeds were justifying him only meant that Abraham's faith by those works revealed a perfected trust in God's faithfulness.

This perfected faith believed God's faithfulness would manifest itself in Isaac's resurrection as we read in Hebrews 11:19, "He considered that God is able to raise men even from the dead." This perfected trust shows itself in values and behaviors that reflect the One you follow. It is the basis of all relationships and friendships.

In Jacob 2:23 Abraham was called a friend of God, and it was proven as he lived out God's values and did what God commanded—not as a legalistic effort, but as shared priorities. We are Messiah's friends when we do what is commanded of us, that is, as we share His values and priorities in our lives (John 15:13-15). In other words, faith explains our deeds and is also a motive for our actions.

There is a fundamental connection between works and faith. Jacob 2:22 says, "You see that faith was *working with* his works, and as a result of his works, faith was perfected." The phrase "working with" is *sunergei* in the Greek which means to cooperate along with faith. Works help to express our living faith.

Maturity of faith is demonstrated when we place God first in all matters. A male baby is a boy from birth, but he becomes a man when he bears the fruit of a man, mature judgment. A pear seed is such intrinsically, but its goal is to bear fruit.

Faith is reckoned as righteousness from the start, but its goal is faithfulness, and good works that reflect a righteous God.

Walking by faith is living out His righteousness, by depending on His Word. By faith in His Word, I am saved. By faith, I now treat my family according to His Word. You cannot say, "Yes, I believe God will save me according to His promise in Yeshua," and at the same time think, "I do not believe He wants me to put my wife's needs before my own." Who do you think you are fooling? His Word applies equally to salvation and our treatment of others.

FAITH IS RECKONED BY GOD'S PERSPECTIVE

The meaning of reckoning: The word "reckoning" is *chashav* in Hebrew. The basic idea of this word is a thinking activity, to consider and esteem. It is the sense of making a judgment or misjudgment. In Isaiah 53:4 the word *chashav* is used for esteem, "We did esteem (*chashav*) him stricken, smitten of God, and afflicted." This same word is then used for "accounting" or crediting to someone's account (Leviticus 25:27, 50, 52; 27:18, 23).

The method of reckoning: In Psalm 32:2, David states, "Blessed is the man to whom the Lord does not imputes (*chashav*) iniquity." In other words, blessed is the man when God does not credit his actions into his sin account. Thus, in doctrinal language:

1. The sin of Adam is imputed to all his descendants. It is reckoned as theirs; therefore they are dealt with as guilty. Sin is sin because it is contrary to God's character, and God therefore imputes it to you as failure; thus, you are a sinner (Psalm 32:1; 2 Timothy 4:16).

2. The righteousness of Messiah is imputed to those who believe in Him. This righteousness is attributed to them as to be considered their own. Thus, the believer in His promises is called righteous, have being made

right with Him. Thus, believers are called "saints."

3. Our sins are imputed to Messiah. He assumed our sinful standing and undertook to answer the demands of justice for our sins. In all these cases the nature of imputation is the same (Romans 5:12-19; cf. Philemon 1:18-19).

God took Abraham's faith and regarded it, estimated it, calculated it, and esteemed it as sufficient ground for receiving him into His favor, considering it to have the value of righteousness which Abraham did not have, for Abraham was a sinner.

The evidence of the righteous standing of God's child is faith; by faith you prove you are God's child. God has decided that faith will be the only spiritual currency He will accept. God takes faith and exchanges it for a heavenly currency, righteousness. A receipt in Hebrew is *cheshbon* (from the same Hebrew word discussed above); a receipt is proof of acquisition and represents that the matter is paid in full. Faith is your receipt proving your righteousness in God's sight, that your (sin) debt is paid in full. The above is stating how you know that God accepts you: "Faith is the assurance" (Hebrews 11:1).

FAITH IS RIGHTEOUSNESS AS GOD'S PROVISION

We may well wonder why God reckoned faith as righteousness. Why not love, mercy, wealth, or coolness (the quality which enables one to sit at the cool kids' table)?

In Hebrew, the word "righteousness" is *tzedakah*. This root means conformity to an ethical or moral standard; in the Bible, that standard is the nature and will of God: "The Lord is righteous in all His ways and holy in all His works" (Psalm 145:17). God's righteous commands are His way of dealing with people. Those who keep His commands are righteous because they live out His values, and they treat people as He would treat them.

Created in God's image, humanity's original state was in righteousness and relating to the righteous God. But sin entered the human equation and our spiritual DNA, so to speak; and with sin in the picture, righteousness was lost, along with our right standing relationship to God. Therefore, the Scripture teaches that no one is righteous, because all have sinned. But the standard for relating to a holy and righteous God has never changed; we are to be holy as He is and not merely as holy as we can be (Leviticus 19:2).

To be declared righteous has always been the hope of our people. We read in Isaiah 45:25: "In the LORD all the offspring of Israel will be justified and will glory." The concept behind the word justified (*tsadek*), or being declared righteous like Abraham, will indeed take place in the future; Israel will trust in Messiah and be made right with God (Zechariah 12:10; 13:1). This is further seen in Isaiah 53:11,

> As a result of the anguish of His soul, He will see *it and* be satisfied; by His knowledge the Righteous One, My Servant, will justify the many, as He will bear their iniquities.

Yes, Messiah, the Righteous Servant, will justify, that is, make many righteous, when they trust in Him. Here is good news for everyone: The Good News of Messiah contains the righteousness of God for all who believe in Yeshua. We read in Romans 1:17, "For in [the Good News] the righteousness of God is revealed from faith to faith; as it is written, 'the just shall live by faith'." In Messiah, all believers in Him are renewed to that righteous state, in order to relate to our righteous God.

This is precisely what the Scriptures affirm: "He who knew no sin, became sin (offering) on our behalf that we might become the righteousness of God in Him" (2 Corinthians 5:21). "Therefore," we are assured, "being justified by faith we have peace with God through our Lord Yeshua the Messiah"

(Romans 5:1).

The power to save you is the Good News of Messiah, faith in Yeshua, the greater seed of Abraham—and that is Good News indeed! Faith relies upon God for what He alone can do, promised to do, and has done in Messiah; this faith is accounted by God, as you doing all righteousness, as you being actually righteous.

It is not faith instead of righteousness. That is, we dare not think that we can be as unrighteous as we want as long as we have faith. Also, it is not faith making your bad deeds good, as if your lie is now true. Nor is faith a magic wand that makes you able to do everything right, as if all you can do now is speak absolute truth and forgive. Righteousness by faith means you have right standing with God, so as to have a right relationship with God.

Abraham and Moses were justified by faith that *anticipated* what God would provide in Messiah. We today are justified by faith that *appropriates* what God has provided in Messiah. All look with the same faith to the same Seed, Savior, and Lord. The same assurance that Abraham is a child of God is our assurance that we are too. He sees us as His righteous children; by faith in Messiah you are a child of God. What confidence we are to have as children, heirs, and conquerors!

The question has come up about whether faith in Messiah Yeshua is necessary to have right standing with God the Father. There are some that take certain New Covenant phrases out of their context in an attempt to prove that sincere, religious Jewish people are in a right relationship with *HaShem* (the Lord) without belief in Messiah. As noted before, Paul testified that in regards to religious Israel, at some of whose hands he suffered, they have "zeal for God, but not according to knowledge" (Romans 10:2). Thus for the Apostles, the "lost sheep of the house of Israel" are not merely secular Jewish people, but are even the most zealous and religious as well.

All people, Jew and Gentile alike, are under "the wrath of God" (Romans 1:18). Only by personal faith in Yeshua are we justified and have "peace with God" (Romans 5:1). However, it is not rejecting Yeshua that damns the soul, for we were all judged. Rather, Yeshua came to save those who were already lost (John 3:17-18).

Messiah, the seed of Abraham, is not only humanity's only hope for a right relationship with God, but it is God's only means of a right relationship with humanity! Faith in Yeshua provides the only righteousness from God to be right with God. In Romans 3:25-26, Paul states that God made this public so that all believers and non-believers in Yeshua would have assurance that there is salvation in none other.

WHEN IS ABRAHAM RECKONED AS RIGHTEOUS?

God reckoned Abraham as righteous in accordance with his faith. Please notice the second "and" (Genesis 15:6). This connects the faith of Abraham and the reckoning by God. There is no accounting of righteousness without actual faith, no salvation without personal faith. No one is saved by the promise without personal faith in that promise.

In Romans 11 of the New Covenant, Paul reminds the Gentile believers in Yeshua that God has not forsaken His people. He assures his readers that God will one day bring a national revival to Israel, where they will nationally trust in Messiah Yeshua; he assures this fact though at that time, as even today, there are mostly broken off natural branches. National Israel is promised salvation, but it only happens when they believe. Paul promises "if they do not continue in their unbelief, they will be grafted in, for God is able to graft them in again" (Romans 11:23).

In Genesis 15:6, the word "reckoned" is in the past tense: It is done! From the moment of faith you are reckoned righteous in Messiah, a child of God! From that moment on, how does God consider you? He reckons you righteous and as His child. Therefore, we should also consider things as God does: I am righteous before Him; I am His child.

Miriam became Mrs. Nadler, my wife, from "I do" onward! When we exchanged our vows, she may not have a total knowledge about her new husband. She may not have known whether I liked beets (I don't!). Nevertheless, she became Mrs. Nadler. Likewise, from the moment of faith, though we all have much to learn about the Lord we have come to trust in, we are children of God.

Self-image issues which stem from sin are to be put to death before God's image. "Even so *consider* yourselves to be dead to sin, but alive to God in Messiah" (Romans 6:11, emphasis mine). "Consider" is the Greek form of the same word for "reckon" in Genesis 15:6. I am reckoned righteous by faith; I am not better than anyone else. The reckoning we are to calculate therefore will affect how I treat others as well, for "love does not take into *account* a wrong suffered" (1 Corinthians 13:5, emphasis mine). As God did not account my sins to me, but instead reckoned me as righteous, so I am not to take into account personal wrong suffered from others. Faith is the key to conquering fear and discouragement, so as to be loving and encouraging to others.

An angry passenger pushed his way to the front of a long line. "I must be on this flight!" he insisted.

The agent replied, "Sure, but I have to take care of these folks first."

The passenger yelled, "Do you have any idea who I am?"

The gate agent said in the public-address microphone,

"Attention, please. We have a passenger here at the gate who does not know who he is. If anyone can help him find his identity, please come to the gate."

Do you have any idea who you are? Some believers do not know who they are, and thus live like who they are not! God has reckoned you righteous and His child by faith in Messiah. You are who God says you are.

5

Faith in Yeshua Alone Saves

Alpha Centauri is located 4.35 light-years from the sun, about a distance of twenty trillion miles and twenty feet (that is, a "20" and twelve zeros). Suppose we had a contest: whoever can jump to Alpha Centauri wins the grand prize! Everyone lines up. I jump about twelve inches. My friend Mike jumps eighteen inches. Michael Jordan jumps about four feet! Try again, Mike: just twenty trillion miles and sixteen feet to go. Gandhi jumps five feet; Martin Luther King, Jr, can jump almost seven feet. Rabbi Zalmon jumps about eighteen feet; only twenty trillion miles left.

Regardless of our progress, we all fall short—way short. Some of us may jump higher, but none can jump high enough. Likewise, you can try reaching up to heaven, but it won't make a difference unless God reaches down to you. Yeshua came, and by faith in Him it's "Hello, Alpha Centauri!"

However, the reality that we fall short of "getting to heaven" is simply an indication of how we fall short right now.

Faith in Messiah Yeshua is the only way—not just to heaven, but also to eternal life now, whether for unbelieving Gentiles or religious Jews. The section of Romans 3:21-31 was meant to teach clearly that there is only one way of salvation.

SALVATION IS OBTAINED BY FAITH

But now apart from the Law the righteousness of God has been manifested, being witnessed by the Law and the Prophets (Romans 3:21).

Salvation is not by works of the Law but by the witness of the Law. Paul proves his argument in Romans 1:18, that all people are under "God's wrath," by showing that attempts to keep the *torah* of Mount Sinai are of no help, because "by the works of the Law no flesh will be justified" (Romans 3:20). Romans 3:21 makes a major transition by stating, "But now," in order to demonstrate that something has recently occurred that was not previously available: the redemption in Messiah. Like a mountain peak that separates east from west, so time is divided by Messiah; all that preceded is past, and the new day has come. In light of what is presently available, "now is the acceptable time" (Isaiah 49:8; 2 Corinthians 6:2).

According to Freiberg's Lexicon, God's righteousness refers to "the divine action by which God puts a person right with himself and which then becomes a dynamic power in the believer's life." Righteousness is a state of always being right with God and accounted as justified in His sight. God's way of making people right with Himself is visibly presented to all mankind through Yeshua.

What people could not do by the Law, God did apart from Law. Even though God's righteousness in Yeshua is not dependent on any works of the *torah* of Moses, the Mosaic *torah* still serves as an eternal purpose in witnessing to this very righteousness. The Law is good, holy, and perfect (Romans 7:12). It rightly demands that we are to be holy as God is holy (Leviticus 19:2). It is like a perfect and holy mirror which reveals our moral imperfections and unholy sin, but cannot make us look better than we are. However, this same holy mirror revealed Yeshua's perfect righteousness. Yeshua fulfilled *torah* like Niagara Falls fills a glass with water.

Paul speaks of "the Law and the Prophets" as witnesses. Leviticus 19:15 requires two witnesses for a valid testimony. Messiah sent His disciples two by two. In the same way, a husband and a wife need to agree for answered prayer (1 Peter 3:7). The Mosaic *torah* required the righteous standard; therefore, the Prophets predicted the righteous Savior. In fact, in Jeremiah 23:6, the prophet states that Messiah is called "the Lord our Righteousness." The righteousness that Mosaic *torah* could not produce in us, was ultimately provided in Messiah.

Therefore, Paul would call it futile and foolish for anyone to think that by doing the works of Law they are made right with God, since the Law itself points us to Yeshua as God's righteousness for all who will believe.

THE CURE FOR FAILURE IS FAITH

> Even the righteousness of God through faith in Yeshua the Messiah for all those who believe; for there is no distinction; for all have sinned and fall short of the glory of God. (Romans 3:22-23)

Salvation is by the faith of sinners, not by the faithfulness of saints. God's righteousness is further defined here as "through faith in Messiah Yeshua," contrasted with works of *torah*-righteousness. The righteousness that God has provided in Messiah does not take effect for anyone apart from personal faith, but rather for everyone who believes in Yeshua, "the surpassing greatness of His power toward us who believe" (Ephesians 1:19).

Faith in Yeshua recognizes the soul's inability to achieve righteousness by one's own efforts and therefore accepts what God bestows. It adds nothing to the gift. A plate resting on the table is doing nothing to hold itself up. Faith contributes nothing, but receives the benefit in full. Messiah's righteousness is accredited to your account when you believe—but not before you believe.

Paul emphasizes that it is for all who believe without distinction. For if even one person—even a very sincere, religious person—could achieve righteousness apart from faith in what God has provided in Messiah, then Yeshua would be an unnecessary and competing means to what was given in the Law.

What God has provided in Yeshua is sufficient for all who believe. There are some in the Messianic world, as well as in the traditional Christian world, who hold to the "unrecognized mediation of Messiah"—that is, sincere religious people are merited salvation by Messiah without the individual ever believing or confessing faith in Yeshua. This is false teaching. God is merciful to all, and that mercy is found in Yeshua for all who will believe. Our actual sins render us guilty, and those without Messiah are still culpable.

An exception is for those who are incapable of making rational, moral choices. Please see how this is noted by Isaiah the prophet:

> He will eat curds and honey at the time he knows to refuse evil and choose good. For before the boy will know to refuse evil and choose good, the land whose two kings you dread will be forsaken. (Isaiah 7:15-16)

In this scenario, the time before a child's ability to "know to choose the good or refuse the evil" is recognized as being a time that the child is not held accountable for his misdeeds. This cannot be said for adults. Adults by definition know right from wrong, and their choosing wrong over right reveals their sinfulness and rebellion to God. The wrong may be by commission (stealing, lying, killing, or slandering Messiah), or it may be by omission (not helping those in need, withholding the truth, not trusting in Messiah). That is why the Scriptures are clear on this matter: "He who believes in the Son has eternal life; but he who does not obey the Son will not see life, but the wrath of God abides on him" (John 3:36; 2 John 9).

In fact, to say that any person has a relationship with God the Father without faith in the Son is contrary to the clear words of Scripture: "Whoever denies the Son does not have the Father; the one who confesses the Son has the Father also" (1 John 2:23).

However, what if they have not heard about Yeshua, especially in a manner in which they can understand the message? True, ignorance of God's will is a mitigating factor—but not to whether people will be judged or not, rather, only to the degree that they will be judged, for they will be judged.

> He will judge the world in righteousness; He will execute judgment for the peoples with equity. (Psalm 9:8)

> And that slave who knew his master's will and did not get ready or act in accord with his will, shall receive many lashes, but the one who did not know it, and committed deeds worthy of a flogging, will receive but few. And from everyone who has been given much, shall much be required; and to whom they entrusted much, of him they will ask all the more. (Luke 12:47-48)

The more you know, the more responsible you are for what you know. However, even someone who does not know, is untaught, or lives in a remote and unreached area, is still responsible for his sins. Ignorance is not an excuse for unbelief and disobedience. God is always fair. "Will not the judge of all the earth do right?" (Genesis 18:25)

Judgment is fair—awful, but fair. No one gets judgment they do not deserve. We all deserve judgment for our sins, for we have offended a holy God, our Creator—whether we live in New York City, Jerusalem, or in the middle of nowhere. It is grace that is "unfair," so to speak.

In Messiah, we receive by grace what we do not deserve—salvation, forgiveness, and heaven. As a holy God, He would be absolutely righteous to allow all to perish, face judgment, and be damned—since we all deserve it. Through His mercy and grace He has provided a Jewish way of salvation for Jew and non-Jew alike—salvation by faith in Messiah Yeshua. It is by faith in Messiah that God demonstrates His grace toward sinners, and this is the righteousness of God. His righteousness is seen in that He has justly dealt with all sin in Messiah. Through faith in Yeshua all believers are saved, acquitted, and declared righteous in Messiah.

Justification declares us righteous. In Greek, "justified" (or declared acquitted) is from a similar root for "righteous." "Justified by faith" means being declared righteous by faith.

Please note that to be declared righteous by faith is distinct from being *made* righteous by faith. The declaration is called justification (detailed out in Romans chapters 3-5); being made righteous by faith is called sanctification (chapters 6-8). Our practical faith response to the grace of God in Messiah is called consecration (chapters 12-15). We are to grow, mature, and develop by grace to become like Messiah, "conformed to the image of the Son" (Romans 8:29).

There are four great truths pertaining to God's righteousness:

1. God is righteous because He is God. His nature is the standard of righteousness.
2. God demands righteousness because He is holy. He cannot allow anything unrighteous in His presence.
3. God provides righteousness in Messiah because He is love. Though holy, He cares for and is committed to lost sinners and desires their fellowship.
4. God develops righteousness because He is the Creator. He created us in His image to relate to Him; as we are conformed to the image of Messiah and spiritually mature we more fully relate to Him.

Many errors develop out of misunderstanding the righteousness of God:

- Paganism lowers God to created things and denies His intrinsic righteous character.
- Legalism develops heresies that teach salvation by works and by our own best efforts. As a result it denies His Holy standard to which none can ever attain.
- Humanism exalts man and denies Yeshua's deity, which makes substitutionary atonement needless.
- Antinomianism or lawlessness confuses justification and sanctification, and therefore denies consecration and practical righteousness.

THE COMPREHENSIVENESS OF FAILURE

Why is salvation only for everyone who will believe? Harry Neale, coach of the Detroit Red Wings and Vancouver Canucks, was once asked about his team's mounting losses. "Last season we couldn't win at home," he replied. "This season we were losing on the road. My failure as a coach is that I can't think of any place else to play." In reality, all of humanity is in the same sinking ship, "for all have sinned" (Romans 3:22b-23). Please note how Paul parallels two phrases to make this perfectly clear: "for all those who believe… for all have sinned."

God has declared that "all have sinned," but this is nothing new, as the *torah* attests in all respects. For example, the Tabernacle veil separated man from God, and it witnessed to the impossibility of approaching God without sacrifice. On *Yom Kippur* (the Day of Atonement), all had to admit their sinfulness by humbling themselves (Leviticus 23:29). Faith was never demonstrated by pleading the keeping of *torah*, but by confessing one's sin and need for blood atonement, forgiveness, and mercy.

The Prophet Isaiah likewise declares that he, along with all Israel, "have gone astray" and that "each has turned to his own way, but that the Lord has laid on Him [Messiah] the iniquity of us all" (Isaiah 53:6). Furthermore the psalmist writes, "there is none that does good, no not one" (Psalm 14:2).

Thus, all *Tanakh*—the *Torah*, the *Nevi'im*, and the *Ketuvim* (Law, Prophets, and the Writings)—testifies to this very truth. We are all sinners and that Messiah is our only hope.

By the same authority that God declares all to be sinners apart from Messiah, He declares us all saints in Messiah. Our security is that there is no difference between the way God implemented in declaring me a sinner and the method He used in declaring me a saint by faith in Yeshua. Faith believes what God has done for us in Messiah. If you can accept with certainty that you are a lost sinner, then accept with that same certainty that you are saved in Yeshua.

Romans 3:23 says, "For all have sinned and fall short of the glory of God." The word, "glory" is *doxa* in the Greek and the root of *doxa* means opinion. It refers to a right opinion about God, that He deserves our praise. The word for "glory" in the Hebrew is *kavod*, which means weight, and it instructs us to give to God what is due to Him, praise and honor.

Being created in His image, we are the only ones of all His creation who could truly appreciate the glory due Him. However, sin separates us from our Creator and renders us unable to live a life that brings Him praise (Isaiah 59:1-2). We failed to live up to His righteous standards and to give Him the praise that He deserves. As a result we are without fellowship with God that He intended for us to enjoy and the glory of His Divine Presence. Due to sin, man lost the privilege he originally had of direct communion with God.

Yeshua brings us back to glory, back to the full weight of God's presence. As we read in Hebrews 2:10, Yeshua is "bringing many sons to glory." Thus, redemption by faith is to be presented gloriously. Preaching is proclamation, not just moralizing. The Good News is not just good advice.

We live in an understandably cynical world. Faith can seem fit only for the naïve and gullible, or as an impossibility for those with any sense of self-respect. When politicians or business executives ask us to just have faith, we snicker and check to see if we still have our wallet. If something seems like it is too good to be true, it probably is; self-reliance is to be valued. Yet despite anyone's cynicism or a desire for self-worth, the Scriptures consistently reveal faith as the basis of any real relationship.

SALVATION IS PROVIDED BY GRACE

Being justified freely by His grace through the redemption which is in Messiah Yeshua. (Romans 3:24)

The phrase, "being justified," is a present-tense, passive verb that refers to being declared righteous. This is not just forgiveness, not just pardoned, not just making up our lack, not just cleansed, but declared righteous, indeed children of God! Our past is pardoned, and our future is secured. Sinners like you and me are justified "freely," that is, as a free gift. It is paid for by Yeshua. Therefore it is ludicrous to think that someone on the basis of their zeal, religious diligence, or sincere efforts could ever earn what God provides by grace in Yeshua.

Grace means unmerited favor. Its not that God sees something in us worth saving; rather, out of pity, mercy, and because He is love, He saves us graciously. The word for "grace" in Greek is *charis*, and this word lies at the basis of the Greek word for joy (*chara*), and for the believer in Messiah Yeshua it leads to thanksgiving (*eucharistia*). Grace leads to graciousness toward others, and gratitude toward God.

Redemption means to buy back, and reflects the biblical idea of being set free, as from the bondage of sin. In His death, Yeshua paid the price to buy me back from darkness: "In Him we have redemption through His blood, the forgiveness of our trespasses, according to the riches of His grace" (Ephesians 1:7).

We are redeemed and set free in Messiah. We are set free with a purpose to live for God. As in Egypt, we were set free to follow God to the place of promise. The free gift of salvation is a freeing gift.

SALVATION IS FOCUSED ON YESHUA

> Whom God displayed publicly as a propitiation in His blood through faith. This was to demonstrate His righteousness, because in the forbearance of God He passed over the sins previously committed; for the demonstration, I say, of His righteousness at the present time, so that He would be just and the justifier of the one who has faith in Yeshua. (Romans 3:25-26)

God's satisfaction for your sin debt is in Messiah's death (Romans 3:25). The word "propitiation" was used to placate or appease. The word is used by the rabbis in the Septuagint (LXX) for *kapporet*, the covering of the ark in the Holy of Holies. This "mercy seat" was a place of atonement, where reconciliation with God was made for our sins. There was no atonement for sins without the shedding of blood (Leviticus 17:11). The *cohen* (priest) would take the atoning blood and sprinkle it on the mercy seat so that the wrath of God would be satisfied (propitiated), and Israel would find mercy and grace in a time of need.

Yeshua is the offering that satisfies God's righteous anger and the full weight of His righteous wrath that we deserved. This is exactly what was promised in the prophets as well:

> But the Lord was pleased to crush Him, putting Him to grief; if He would render Himself as a guilt offering, He will see His offspring, He will prolong His days, and the good pleasure of the Lord will prosper in His hand. As a result of the anguish of His soul, He will see it and be satisfied; by His knowledge the Righteous One, My Servant, will justify the many, as He will bear their iniquities. (Isaiah 53:10-11)

By saying that Yeshua's death is the propitiation, it is saying that Yeshua is the place of atonement. The mercy seat is no longer kept in the sacred seclusion of the most holy place: It is displayed before the eyes of all. Messiah is the meeting place of God and man where the mercy of God is available because of the sacrifice of the Son. God's desired reconciliation with a lost humanity, of Jews and Gentiles alike, is in Messiah's death.

HIS PERFECT WORK PROVES FORBEARANCE OF GOD

What about Abraham, Moses, and David? They sinned, but they were saved. The full penalty for sin was not exacted from our believing ancestors; this was in line with God's forbearance. Forbearance speaks of God's patience, knowing His justice would be satisfied in Yeshua. He provided altars and sacrifices which covered over the sins (*kippur* literally means "covered"). They all were saved looking to what Messiah would fully provide. What was covered then is now fully removed through Yeshua's atonement. All the types and sacrifices were promissory notes that Yeshua's atonement paid off and that is why "Abraham was glad to see His day" (John 8:56). What they anticipated by faith we now appropriate by faith.

Ever notice how companies will take out ads in magazines and newspapers declaring publicly that a class action lawsuit has been settled? They want everyone to know that the debt has been paid and that they are now in good standing with the public. Though we were the ones that had a sin debt with God, Yeshua was the one who paid the debt and has publicly declared that by faith in Him we are in good standing with God.

HIS PERFECT WORK PROVES THAT FORGIVENESS OF SINNERS IS NOT WICKEDNESS

God is not only just, but also the justifier. Yeshua is the public declaration that God is at once just in His character and justifying in His conduct on our behalf. He is just because He is holy; He is justifying because He is love. Yeshua satisfies all the holy demands of God. The very Judge who pronounced us guilty then took the penalty upon Himself so that He could righteously pronounce us free. If God had forgiven sinners without the payment for sins, it would be like a judge allowing criminals to get off without judgment—and that would be seen as evil! Messiah's perfect work satisfies God and man. Yeshua is God's public demonstration that all is forgiven, and we can come home.

There is a story of a boy who stole from his folks and humiliated them. Out of guilt and shame he ran away from home. Several years later he wrote his dad and said, "I will be in your area; if I can come by and if you want me back, leave the porch light on. But if you don't think it right, I will understand—because I know I am not worthy and embarrassed you publicly, and I do not deserve your acceptance." It was signed, "Your son, Phil." When Phil got to his old neighborhood, he was almost afraid to go near. But when he saw his home, he did not see the porch light on. Instead they had lit every light in the house and had put up extra lights around the house. It looked like a brilliant, glorious temple. The whole town could see the shining light. He later asked his dad, "Why did you do that?" "I didn't want any doubt in your mind, or in anyone else's, that I forgive you: Welcome home son." There is no doubt about it for you. You are forgiven. God publicly manifested and displayed His righteousness to set you free. We are His lights in the darkness, His demonstration models declaring that which we have received: God has publicly forgiven you in Yeshua. There is no shame in coming home.

FAITH IN YESHUA ALONE EXTOLS THE ETERNAL LORD

Justification by faith fights the spiritual war on three fronts: inwardly, regarding myself; outwardly, regarding others; eternally, regarding the Lord. There are also exclusionary results of redemption by faith: inwardly, pride is excluded and outwardly, prejudice is excluded. We are not to develop pride, but develop lowliness. We are not to allow haughtiness, but rather acceptance of others. And we are not to be loveless, but act in all submission and obedience to the authority of God, not permitting lawlessness toward Him.

PRIDE IS EXCLUDED

Where then is boasting? It is excluded. By what kind of law? Of works? No, but by a law of faith. For we maintain that a man is justified by faith apart from works of the Law. (Romans 3:27-28)

The word "boasting" is referring to trusting in ourselves for our salvation. Simply put, the law of faith removes pride. But what is wrong with boasting and taking pride in what you have accomplished? When entering the land we were warned by God about this same matter:

> Beware that you do not forget the Lord your God by not keeping His commandments and His ordinances and His statutes which I am commanding you today; otherwise, when you have eaten and are satisfied, and have built good houses and lived in them, and when your herds and your flocks multiply, and your silver and gold multiply, and all that you have multiplies, then your heart will become proud and you will forget the Lord your God who brought you out from the land of Egypt, out of the house of slavery. He led you through the great and terrible wilderness, with its fiery serpents and scorpions and thirsty ground where there was no water; He brought water for you out of the rock of flint. In the wilderness He fed you manna which your fathers did not know, that He might humble you and that He might test you, to do good for you in the end. Otherwise, you may say in your heart, "My power and the strength of my hand made me this wealth." But you shall remember the Lord your God, for it is He who is giving you power to make wealth, that He may confirm His covenant which He swore to your fathers, as it is this day (Deuteronomy 8:11-18).

Satan had this same problem of self-centered pride (Isaiah 14:12-14; Ezekiel 28:12-19; 1 Timothy 3:6; 1 John 2:16).

Boastful pride is self-exalting and foolish, for we have nothing that we have not received from God. Pride is a symptom of our rebellion and sinful separation from our Creator. It is not that God is greedy and does not want to share the glory. Scripture declares that "Salvation is of the Lord" (Jonah 2:10) and not of our works.

Sinful pride in our own deeds is removed only by faith. This is why boasting is excluded. Some people have the false idea that before Yeshua, the Law saved people by works. This is wrong. The law of Moses (*torah*) is not a law of works, but a law of faith. This is what Paul had been teaching through this whole letter to the Romans:

> For in the gospel a righteousness from God is revealed, a righteousness that is by faith from first to last, just as it is written: "The righteous will live by faith." (Romans 1:17)

For Paul, the Mosaic *torah* is a *torah* of faith. This portion in Romans 1:17 is taken from Habakkuk 2:4, and it is repeated elsewhere in the New Covenant Scriptures (in Galatians 3:11; Hebrews 10:38). In the Talmud, we read how Rabbi Simlai, in the third century, noted 365 prohibitions and 248 positive commands within Moses. Then David, in Psalm 15, reduced them to eleven. Then Isaiah made them six (Isaiah 33:14-15), and Micah 6:8 binds them into three. The rabbincal discussion concludes:

> Again came Isaiah and reduced them to two [principles], as it is said "Thus saith the Lord, [i] Keep ye justice and [ii] do righteousness." ... But it is Habakkuk who came and based them all on one, namely—"The just shall live by his faith." (Makkot 23b-24a; Isaiah 66:1; Habakkuk 2:4)

The New Covenant is not in contradiction to the *torah* of Moses, but it is the fulfillment of all the *torah* of Moses anticipated. That is why Paul states that the righteousness of God by faith in Messiah is witnessed to by the Law and the prophets (Romans 3:21).

The Mosaic *torah* directed a believer's faith to Yeshua, and it still does (Galatians 3:22-24). *Torah* not only included sacrifices for sin, but it also said that all needed to trust in that bloody provision of God for their atonement. Therefore, *torah* never permitted anyone to boast in their own works, but condemned such boasting as sin.

Those who are righteous by faith declare with the Psalmist, "My soul will make its boast in the Lord" (Psalm 34:2). Paul also repeats these words in 1 Corinthians 1:31, "Let him who boasts, boast in the Lord." As opposed to the self-righteous, "The boastful shall not stand before Your eyes; You hate all who do iniquity" (Psalm 5:5). And so the prophet Jeremiah writes:

> Thus says the Lord, "Let not a wise man boast of his wisdom, and let not the mighty man boast of his might, let not a rich man boast of his riches; but let him who boasts boast of this, that he understands and knows Me, that I am the Lord who exercises lovingkindness, justice, and righteousness on earth; for I delight in these things," declares the Lord (Jeremiah 9:23-24).

If any are justified by God, it is by faith alone, so no one could boast. A message of faith is not contrary to *torah*, but quite the opposite: it is the fulfillment of *torah*. Self-centered pride is dependent on works for a sense of self-worth. By contrast, faith finds full acceptance in what God has accomplished in Yeshua. In Messiah, we are children of God.

Faith and pride cannot coexist because they are mutually exclusive. Works are self-congratulatory; faith is God-glorifying. Romans 3:28 begins with the word "for" to demonstrate the reason for Paul's working principle of faith. All "law-works," any rules you live by which you hope will justify you, are excluded. All self-centered works are barred, excluded from adding anything to our account before God. Therefore, accurate teaching of Scripture regarding this matter of faith produces humility, not haughtiness, in the believer. Faith is victorious when it exalts the Lord, not self.

Paul writes that justification is "apart from works of *torah*." We usually call traditionally religious Jews "observant" because they observe and give heed to the commandments (*mitzvot*). The phrase, "works of the Law," is the equivalent of being observant. Works do not commend you spiritually since they always reveal how far we fall short; dependence on them is vain, since it does not bring us closer to salvation.

There is an old illustration for this: California is beautiful and diverse; it has the lowest spot in the USA (Death Valley) and the highest spot (Mt. Whitney). But whether you are living in either place, you are still in California! Similarly, in the state of spiritual death we tend to judge those who are evidently criminals and approve of those that seem to help others. Though the two may be vastly different in the eyes of people, God knows that we all fall short of His glory. So whether you are robbing a bank or helping little old ladies across the street to win your merit badge, you are still dead in your sins and trespasses. You must come out of death, not merely ascend in death. So let us therefore boast in the Lord, for faith excludes all boasting in self.

PREJUDICE IS EXTINGUISHED

> Is God the God of Jews only? Is He not the God of Gentiles also? Yes, of Gentiles also, since indeed God who will justify the circumcised by faith and the uncircumcised through faith is one (Romans 3:29-30)

In Romans 3:29, Paul declares that salvation by works is renounced by the very nature of God: He is one! Sound familiar? It should, we declare this every Shabbat: "*Shema Israel Adonai Eloheinu Adonai echad*! Hear O Israel, the Lord our God, the Lord is one!" Paul's point is simple: Since there is only one God, then there is only way to be saved. There is no other way of salvation. However, some do teach that there are two ways of salvation: the *torah* of Moses for the Jews and Yeshua for the Gentiles. This is not true. There is only one way to be saved. God graciously saves all people by faith in Yeshua. God is not merely the national treasure of Israel, but the universal Lord of all. Gentile believers may now say, "For You are our Father, though Abraham does not know us, and Israel does not recognize us. You, O Lord, are our Father, our Redeemer from of old is Your name" (Isaiah 63:16).

In Romans 3:30, Paul further declares that salvation by works is renounced by the need of man. Paul writes that faith "will justify." This the way of salvation, not only now (Romans 3:21), but in the future, and forever! The reason is that all are in the same dire need. If you had a Jersey cow and a Holstein, and the Jersey gives more butterfat, it is more valuable. But if both cows are infected with Tuberculosis, both are of no value at all. And using a centrifuge to separate the cream from the skimmed milk ("Maybe I can at least sell the cream," you think) will not help – it is all infected, it is all wasted. Likewise the religious and the irreligious, the educated and the ignorant, Jewish or Gentile – all are lost and need the same salvation by grace through faith in Yeshua. Let Jews boast that God is saving Gentiles. Let Gentiles boast that God is saving Jews! There is no room for pride or prejudice. If we are living by faith, we are not judging by the flesh (2 Corinthians 5:16).

We are told "there is salvation in no one else; for there is no other name under heaven that has been given among men by which we must be saved" (Acts 4:12). God is the Father of all who believe, and all believers are true family in Messiah. Faith is victorious when it accepts others as we have been accepted in Messiah. Faith excludes all pride, but it includes all people. Faith alone represents the love of God.

Part Two

God's Calling for Messianic Gentiles

Praise the Lord, all nations;
Laud Him, all peoples!

For His lovingkindness is great towards us,
And the truth of the Lord is everlasting.

Psalm 117:1-2

6

The Gentile Great Commission

Having considered God's heart for His people and the necessity of Messianic congregations oriented around faith in Yeshua, we will now consider God's radical call for Gentiles within the Messianic testimony. Strange as it may seem today, the earliest believers in Yeshua assumed that Gentile believers were to become Jews. Thus, it was initially thought that they needed to be circumcised (Acts 11:1-3; 15:1, 5). Indeed, the issue of Gentile circumcision was not resolved until the Jerusalem council (Acts 15). A Gentile like Cornelius who came to faith in Judea before this time would probably have found himself on the business end of a *mohel*'s blade.

Even after it was decided that Gentile believers did not have to become Jews and submit to circumcision, Jewish believers continued to be circumcised (Acts 16:1-3). Such an act, for Jewish believers, testified that the Abrahamic covenant was still in force in Messiah (Galatians 3:17). But the issue of Gentile circumcision was bound up with the larger issues of Jewish-Gentile interaction, stemming from the portions of the *Tanakh* which forbade intermarriage between believers and non-believers (Genesis 24:2-9; Deuteronomy 7:3). If for example, a woman married an uncircumcised man, she would take on the religious values of the husband, which would lead to apostasy.

An implication for Jews, then, was to have no social relations with the uncircumcised. In fact, no uncircumcised males could share in a Passover meal (Exodus 12:48). The issue of Gentile believers in the family of faith was a dicey one.

Today with the resurgence of the Messianic testimony, the questions regarding Jews and Gentiles together in Messiah have again become controversial, and with good reason. Not long ago, Jews who came to believe in Yeshua were considered "former Jews," and expected to take on the expression of faith and practice of the religion which was thought to have replaced Judaism. Of course, this assumption remains for many. Yet now, with the growth of a community where Yeshua-faith is once again lived out from a Biblical Jewish frame of reference, the question of Gentile inclusion must be reconsidered.

How do congregations maintain the truth of equality in Yeshua, without losing distinctive Jewish identity, and without pressuring Gentiles to become Jews or think of themselves as such? Should it be said, as some have assumed, that Messianic Jewish congregations are for Jews and intermarrieds, but not Gentiles? Should Gentiles be considered members and participate in community life (marriage, *Bar Mitzvah*, etc.)? Should they be in leadership?

We have already considered that salvation and righteousness is based upon faith in Yeshua for both Jews and Gentiles. As it turned out, most Jewish people did not come to faith, and many more Gentiles came to believe on Yeshua. Over time, Gentile cultural expression of the faith became dominant along with Gentile attendance. Therefore, the question was raised: doesn't more Gentiles than Jews coming to faith in Yeshua mean that God has rejected the Jews? Romans 11 was meant to answer this critical question. If God could forsake the Jewish people to whom He had made so many promises, then who could ever be secure in promises from a God who breaks His Word (Jeremiah 31:31-37)?

We've seen in previous chapters why the question matters. But Paul's answer is significant in how it includes, not only the Jewish people, but all peoples. In context, Paul gives two evidences of God's faithfulness. The first piece comes in the beginning of the chapter (Romans 11:1-10). The faithfulness of God is seen in the Jewish remnant according to grace. Paul views himself (11:1), along with the testimony of Elijah (11:2-4) and all Jewish believers at "this present time" (11:5-6), as constituting one proof of God's faithfulness, that He has not rejected His people. In light of the Jewish remnant, we see that Israel's national unbelief is only partial (11:1-10). This remnant is the guarantee, the down payment as it were, of the future national revival.

However, if that's the case for Jews, how do the Gentiles fit into God's saving plan? In fact, Paul argues, the believing Gentiles were to be the second piece of evidence regarding God's faithfulness to Israel.

> I say then, they did not stumble so as to fall, did they? May it never be! But by their transgression salvation has come to the Gentiles, to make them jealous. Now if their transgression is riches for the world, and their failure is riches for the Gentiles, how much more will their fulfillment be! But I am speaking to you who are Gentiles. Inasmuch then as I am an apostle of Gentiles, I magnify my ministry, if somehow I might move to jealousy my fellow countrymen and save some of them. For if their rejection is the reconciliation of the world, what will their acceptance be, but life from the dead? (Romans 11:11-15)

Israel's national failure to accept Messiah Yeshua gave an opportunity for all believers to be concerned for Israel's national revival. Thus, Israel's national unbelief is not only partial, but also temporary, and the Gentile believers are key to how temporary their national unbelief will be (11:11-24). The faithfulness of God is evidenced by the Gentile believers' call to make Israel jealous (11:11-32).

A REDEMPTIVE PURPOSE FOR GENTILE BELIEVERS

Our confidence in God's Word and its sure fulfillment will impact our evangelistic activities (11:11-15), as well as our eternal perspective (11:16-25). Therefore, Paul teaches that the fulfillment of Israel's national revival is certain because God's calling is irrevocable (11:25-29). Nevertheless it will be fulfilled when Gentiles minister to Jewish people the same mercy that they have received (11:30-32). Since the failure of Israel is partial (11:1-10), and the fall of Israel is temporary (11:11-24), we know that the fulfillment of Israel is certain (11:25-29).

In this chapter we will consider Romans 11:11-15, where Paul says that the faithfulness of God is evidenced in the Gentile believers' life of faith, a life that will make Israel jealous unto salvation.

> I say then, they did not stumble so as to fall, did they? May it never be! But by their transgression salvation has come to the Gentiles, to make them jealous." (Romans 11:11)

Indeed, Israel stumbled over Messiah. This is an indirect reference to the Messiah as the stumbling stone (Romans 9:32-33). To stumble and fall can make for great comedy. In an episode of the American version of *The Office*, we see Kevin Malone (played by Brian Baumgartner) carrying a giant pot of chili into the work area. As he proudly describes his family's recipe in the voice-over, the camera shows him awkwardly stumbling and falling over. The gargantuan pot of chili spills all over the work-area and himself. As surprisingly low-brow the gag is, the audience cannot help but laugh at the combination of this poor sight of Kevin's stumble contrasted with his proud description of culinary accomplishment.

How does God feel about people who stumble? Some Gentile believers were arrogant against Israel. These believers therefore neglected their responsibility to reach out to the Jewish people in love (Romans 11:18). As the "apostle of Gentiles,"

Paul needed to take them to task. They were not to have an "I told you so" attitude toward the Jewish people.

Did Israel's stumbling over Messiah mean their utter ruin? From a Jewish perspective, Gentile believers seem to think so. Once I was asked to speak at a church in Kiev, Ukraine, at an outreach around the time of the Jewish revival in the former Soviet Union. I was one of three speakers. The speaker before me told the Jewish people who were visiting, "You Jews missed it—and too bad for you! Sunday is the Sabbath now!" How bizarre, both for the theology and in the attitude reflected. In America, a pastor told me that "when we go door-to-door to share the Gospel, we skip the homes with mezuzahs. We would not want to offend [the Jews living there], our people would not know what to say, and they probably would not be interested anyway." Shouldn't the Jewish homes have been offended that they were skipped? This non-witness, though well-intentioned, actually assumes that God is finished with Israel.

You may have rejected God; but God has not rejected you. The proof is that God calls out to you to be saved through the proclamation of the Good News of Messiah. God's faithfulness to Israel is evidenced in Jewish evangelism, whereas not witnessing to the Jewish people implies that God has rejected Israel. Why do Gentile believers misunderstand this? They do not understand their calling from God to reach out to Israel with the Good News.

Who purposed Gentile believers to make Israel jealous? It was God's purpose. Did Israel's stumbling mean their utter collapse? They did fall (Romans 11:22). Yet their total ruin was not God's purpose, but rather He used their weakness to help others.

Stumbling was Israel's own doing, their own response to His message. Yet God's purpose in all these things was to bring salvation to the nations—it always was (Genesis 12:3). God is good; He never sets us up to fall. We fall of our own foolishness.

We are not born unlucky, under a bad sign, or cursed by God. Rather, our stumbling is meant for us to see our need for His grace and mercy. Anyone can stumble, and everyone has, but the repentant sinner can be restored (Ephesians 2:5; Colossians 2:13). This is the Good News for you and national Israel.

In God's foreknowledge, He purposed that the Good News would go to the Gentiles by means of national Israel's unbelief. He purposed to utilize Israel's weakness. If God is so good and foreknowing, why would He create a world where there is weakness at all? Because He desired to create free creatures to share in His glory. The downside of free will is that we can do some very weak, stupid things with it—like rejecting Messiah. And sadly, people's minds are darkened by their sin against God (Romans 1:21).

This condition is not unique to Jews, any more than salvation is a completely Gentile affair. Thus Paul's argument began with the fact that there is a Jewish remnant representing Israel and evidencing God's faithfulness to His people (Romans 11:1-10). Salvation has come to the Gentiles, as well as the Jewish people.

We may have presumed that our chosenness meant we already had a relationship with God. In our pride, we may not have realized our own desperate need for salvation from sin. Thus, the majority's failure to accept Messiah, even as the Gentiles were believing on Him, put us in a place to see what we stumbled over as the very thing we desperately need. But how do the Gentiles help Jewish people see this?

Consider Sara and Millie. Sara was always well dressed and thought little of her neighbor, the plain and shabbily dressed Millie. One day, they were both in a clothing store at the same time. Sara had passed by a rack of coats, but Millie stopped to try one on. Sara noticed Millie in the full-length mirror, admiring the coat, and exclaimed, "I saw that first!" "Then why did you pass on it when you first saw it?" Millie responded.

"I didn't think much of it until I saw it on you," Sara replied. "If it makes you look that good, then I really need it as well!" As Gentiles are 'clothed' in Yeshua, the very Jewish Messiah, with all the love and joy He brings, our people will be made jealous for the Messiah of Israel. The Gentiles are to demonstrate Messiah and the blessings in Him so that Israel would be provoked to jealousy.

Some may ask, "You don't mean to say that God saved Gentiles just to make Israel jealous, do you?" No, not quite. God saves Gentiles because of who He is, as it is written, "for God so loved the world He gave His only begotten Son" (John 3:16). However, our salvation gives us a purpose and a calling. Even as God saved Gentiles through the means of Israel's transgression, He now gives Gentile believers an opportunity to demonstrate God's faithfulness to Israel. God intended the Good News to come to the Jewish people through faithful Gentile believers.

Often we do not see Jewish people all that jealous for what the Gentile believer has in Messiah. Why? God gets jealous over Israel when they go after other gods (Exodus 34:14). This is because Israel belongs to Him. By contrast, how can Jewish people get jealous over something that is not evidently theirs to begin with? Though some may be curious or even a little envious, Jewish people do not rightfully get jealous over Easter eggs or Santa Claus, because they are not part of Jewish heritage, and instead function as a cultural substitute for that heritage. On the contrary, when believers worship the Lord Yeshua, rejoicing in the Messiah and God of Israel, this should provoke Israel to jealousy.

Has the Jewish people's rich inheritance in Messiah been disguised? Many times Christian culture seems alien. Even thinking of visiting a church can seem a little like asking men to meet in the Ladies' room! How would Paul, the Apostle to the Gentiles feel about this matter? I believe he might ask, "Why are you trying to be culturally different than the

Jewish community? Your liberty in Yeshua was meant to help you identify with Israel, not be alienated from them! It is the God of Israel you have come to know, but through the cultural expression of your faith the Jewish community can not recognize Him!"

At Antioch, when Gentiles came to faith and were first called *christianoi* ("Christians," Acts 11:26), the term identified them with the Messiah ("Anointed One" in Greek). Think of it: to the ears of the Jewish community, which generally spoke Greek outside Judea, the Gentile "Christians" were really "Messianics": they were a part of the Messianic Jewish community. In other words, unlike today, this term did not separate them out as a foreign religion; rather, it identified them with Israel. Messianic Gentiles were meant to be the living witness of Israel's hope. God's salvation leads to a service of love.

RICHES FOR THE GENTILE BELIEVERS

Now if their transgression is riches for the world, and their failure is riches for the Gentiles, how much more will their fulfillment be!" (Romans 11:12)

There are riches for the Gentile world that result from their witness to Israel. What kind of riches does Paul speak about? Don't believers already have the great riches and eternal blessings we receive by faith in Messiah, salvation and eternal glory (Romans 9:23; 10:12; Ephesians 1:7; 2:7; Colossians 1:27)? Is there something more? Indeed.

The word "fulfillment" (or "fullness" as in some translations) refers to the national salvation of Israel by faith in Messiah. The word "fullness" is the Greek word *playroma*, and it means complete or fulfilled, as in "complete in Messiah" (Colossians 2:9-10). In contrast to there only being a remnant, this refers to a national revival when Israel will obey the Good News and come to faith as a nation. It will mark an end to the state of hardening that now characterizes most Jewish people in regards to the Good News (Romans 11:25).

The people being fulfilled are indicated by the possessive pronoun "their" in Romans 11:12; this specifically refers to the ones "hardened" (7). Later on, these same "hardened" ones will be characterized as "broken off" branches (in Romans 11:17-24). God's purpose will be fully realized at the time of the Jewish people's "fulfillment."

Fulfillment contrasts with transgression. We were told as a people to trust in Yeshua and obey Him, but as a people we did not (cf. "disobedience" in Romans 11:30-31). When Israel believes and obeys Yeshua, they fulfill God's will for them (as in Acts 3:19-21). Thus the national hardening is not only partial, but also temporary. When we are not disobedient, we will be fulfilled: the fullness of Israel will have come in!

In general, the Gentile body of Messiah thinks they are doing fine without focusing on Jewish ministry. But what is God's revealed will? There is more, indeed, "how much more will their fulfillment be!" (Romans 11:12, emphasis mine).

Paul is trying to encourage Gentiles that it is in their best interests to seek Israel's fulfillment in their expression of faith. This will bring about the blessings of God's fulfilled plan for Jews and Gentiles. This "investment" has a guaranteed return.

This chapter in Romans reveals God's plan for Israel's restoration. His plan for Gentile fulfillment is inextricably tied to Israel's fulfillment (Romans 11:12, 15). The Greek word for "fullness" as regarding Israel in Romans 11:12 is the same exact Greek word for the "fullness of the Gentiles" in Romans 11:25, which we will study in chapter 8. Even as completeness for Israel in regards to God's plan for Israel is restoration of the nation by their looking to Yeshua, God's plan for completeness for the Gentile believers is for them to make Israel jealous so that Israel will be restored to God.

How do you get more blessing? Giving away love is how you receive it. It is like my dad's fan principle. The small New York City apartment we lived in was without air-conditioning. His solution was to turn the fan around so that it was blowing out of the window, and then open another window, which would cause the air to be drawn into the apartment. This brought a fresh breeze. Giving away love and faith is how you get more. God's way of increasing the blessings you receive is by you reaching out. It is always more blessed to give than receive.

THE GENTILE BELIEVERS' CALLING

> But I am speaking to you who are Gentiles. Inasmuch then as I am an apostle of Gentiles, I magnify my ministry, if somehow I might move to jealousy my fellow countrymen and save some of them." (Romans 11:13-14)

Paul says, "I am speaking," not "I will be speaking." In other words, he was already speaking to the Gentiles through the entire chapter. There are some who teach (and many who believe) that once a Gentile comes to faith in Messiah, he or she is no longer a Gentile, but is now a spiritual Jew (or spiritual "Israel"). Paul is quite clear on this point: Just as Jews that believe in Yeshua are still Jews (Romans 9:3-4; 11:1), so Gentiles who believe in Messiah are still Gentiles. For the sake of political correctness, many believers might be tempted to ask, "Why does he bother to say that? Shouldn't we just forget about any differences, since we're all one in Messiah?" Yes, we are one in Messiah, but that unity is spiritual and entails our diversity as well. We must be careful not to exchange unity for uniformity, disregarding our diversity in Messiah. Paul wanted Gentile believers to reach out to the Jewish people as Gentiles, and not by calling themselves Jews.

The Apostle authorizes outreach to Israel as a practice of Gentiles and their disciples. His saying that he magnifies his ministry is not implying that he is arrogant, but rather Paul meant to especially encourage Gentile believers in reaching out to the Jewish people. Why "as Gentiles"? Paul wanted to show that the Abrahamic Covenant was fulfilled in Yeshua, the greater seed of Abraham (Galatians 4:16).

This covenant not only assured Abraham that he would have a Land and a Seed (Genesis 12:1-2, 7; 15:5), but also that all the families of the earth would be blessed through his seed (Genesis 12:3; 22:18). As Paul describes it:

> In order that in Messiah Yeshua the blessing of Abraham might come to the Gentiles, so that we would receive the promise of the Spirit through faith (Galatians 3:14).

Gentile ministry to the Jewish people is evidence of the fulfillment of the Abrahamic Covenant in Yeshua, a testimony to Israel that Yeshua is the Messiah. This also explains why Paul was willing to give up his life, and certainly his freedom, to bring the financial gift from the Gentiles to the Jewish people in Jerusalem (1 Corinthians 16:3; Romans 15:25-27; Acts 21:11-13). This gift would be the first fruits of what God had promised in the prophets (Isaiah 2:3; 60:1-6). The testimony of love from the Gentiles by sharing Messiah with Israel in a culturally relevant, yet clear manner, would be proof that God has not forsaken Israel at all. Rather, Messiah Yeshua is the very fulfillment of the hope of Israel. He is God's faithfulness to Israel.

Paul says, "I had been entrusted with the Gospel to the uncircumcised, just as Peter had been to the circumcised" (Galatians 2:7). Some may get confused over this division of apostolic labor between Peter and Paul. There were not two different works of God, that is, a work among the Jewish people and a work among the Gentiles. There is only one work of God, to demonstrate God's faithfulness to Israel. Peter's work was directly to the Jews; Paul's was indirectly to the Jews through the Gentiles. The two men worked to reach Israel in different ways.

Gentile believers must embrace their calling as Gentiles to make Israel jealous by mercy and love. Stop waiting for some special calling before you reach out to the Jewish people with the Good News of Messiah. Every believer is called to and responsible for demonstrating God's faithfulness to Israel. Even as all ministries are to be oriented "to the Jew first," all may "magnify their ministry," whatever that specific ministry may be (Romans 11:13).

Romans 11:14 is one of my favorite verses: "if somehow I might move to jealousy my fellow countrymen and save some of them." I love the sense of desperation in the phrase, "if somehow." It communicates Paul's sense of urgency; he used various creative methods to reach out to the Jewish people. In essence, Paul is saying, "If I don't do everything to see that my ministry to the Gentiles is effectively reaching out to the Jewish people, then I'm dishonoring my calling and office."

The job of Gentile ministry is not merely to give a token effort to Jewish ministry, but to reveal God's desperate love for Israel and all lost people. If one approach does not work (or even if it does), we try another, even being "all things to all men, as a Jew as unto the Jews" that some might be saved (1 Corinthians 9:20-22). This is the forgotten mission of believers generally, one which has been relegated to a table at a missions conference.

I notice that some Gentile believers wear a Jewish Star necklace at work or elsewhere. Others have considered them "wannabe Jews," or thought that wearing the jewelry will at least give off that impression. However, such behavior, rather than reflecting a confused identity, can reflect a renewed sense of mission. I myself recently suggested to someone, "try wearing a Jewish Star at work. If you are asked about it, you'll have an opportunity to explain that your Savior is Jewish, and about the hope, forgiveness, and joy that you experience because of the Jewish Messiah." Even simple things may have a new purpose in context.

However, our calling needs to go below the surface. It must be the practice of every Gentile believer and of all congregations to do all they can to make Israel jealous for Messiah. Paul knew it was God's will for Israel to be saved, therefore he did all he could to fulfill God's will in both prayer and practice (Romans 10:1). That's what believing God's will is supposed to accomplish in us.

I met Miriam when she came out to the West coast to attend a mutual friend's wedding. It was just a few weeks after I had come to faith, and things between us progressed slowly over the next year. However, once I believed it was God's will for me to marry her and no one else, I knew I had to win her "by any means." I interrogated someone who I thought might also be interested in her, asking him "what are your intentions towards Miriam?" I even took up Israeli folk dancing, though I am not a dancer, and was not really interested in this strange behavior. My motivation was to do whatever I could to be with her.

Paul also did all he could. In Antioch, Paul "sat in the synagogue" and waited to be called upon to speak before saying anything (Acts 13:14-15). Elsewhere, he initiated action and boldly preached in the marketplaces "to anyone that happened to be present" (Acts 17:17). There were no printing presses, Good News pamphlets, newspapers, radios, television, or internet—so he reached the crowds as best he could. In Ephesus, he taught "both publicly and house-to-house" (Acts 20:20). In general, Paul made himself to be as a "servant to all" for the sake of the Good News "that I may become a fellow partaker of it" (1 Corinthians 9:19, 23).

LIBERTY TO SERVE

What about a believer's liberty to live and worship as he or she wishes? There is no such thing. We worship as God has revealed in accordance with the Scriptures; we live as He called us to live, in accordance with the Scriptures. The liberty we have in Messiah is so that we might be more faithful to Messiah in reaching out with Good News, not to justify our personal preferences.

We should never use our liberty if it would keep Jewish people from understanding the Good News. Perhaps we need to re-evaluate the cultural expression of worship and witness and see if it is communicating clearly to people outside the faith, or if it merely reinforces Gentile tradition. Let us pray about how to change our cultural expressions to more effectively communicate to all with ears to hear, even to the Jew first.

I appreciate Paul's final comment in Romans 11:14, "and save some of them." Paul knew that only God can save people, but he identifies his call as God's instrument of grace. In that sense, he co-labors with Messiah (2 Corinthians 6:1).

Paul was certain of God's promises, and therefore could say that at a future time "all Israel will be saved" (Romans 11:26). Why does he say merely "some of them"? He understood that he would see a remnant; it may be comparatively few Jews who will be saved in the present. However, these few are the foregleams of the national restoration of the future. Let's not over-hype or raise expectations to an unreasonable level, and then exaggerate the results. Not every movie, shroud, concert, or ossuary is going to bring revival! Let us, along with Paul, say, "If by any means I may move to jealousy the Jewish people and save some of them" (1 Corinthians 9:22; Romans 11:14).

It is essential that Jewish people in congregations discipled responsibly, so that they will be effective witnesses as Jews back to their Jewish family and community. So also Gentiles, like Ruth, you have been joined to Israel (Ruth 1:16-17). You are also responsible to be discipled and disciple others in such a way that you will be effective witnesses as Gentiles, back to your Jewish family.

Many congregations or churches are concerned that they will be compromising their commitment to biblical truth by adjusting their cultural expression. We should, of course, never compromise the truth of Scripture or water down the Good News, in order to merely make it more appealing to others.

However the God of Creation is still able to give us creative ideas to communicate His truth effectively without diminishing the truth. In the incarnation, Yeshua came into the "likeness of sinful flesh" without compromising God's holiness, righteousness, and love (Romans 8:3; Philippians 2:5-8). Therefore, I am convinced that, like Paul, we too can communicate the truth of Messiah without compromising our biblical values. We must never confuse our cultural expression with the truth itself and end up defending our culture rather than the faith.

REJECTION AND RESURRECTION

For if their rejection is the reconciliation of the world, what will their acceptance be, but life from the dead? (Romans 11:15)

We have seen the Gentile witness to Israel takes real priority in Gentile ministry. Here Paul elaborates by making a remarkable comparison, looking first at "their rejection"—again, Israel's rejection. But we need to clear up an ambiguity in translating this verse. The King James Version reads, "For if the casting away of them be the reconciling of the world..." Similarly, the New King James Version reads, "For if their being cast away is the reconciling of the world..." Both of these versions say that Israel (to whom "their" refers in 11:15) was cast away.

Other versions read, "For if their rejection is the reconciliation of the world" (NIV; NASB; NET; NRSV). In these versions, "their rejection" translates the Greek in a literal way.

So, who is doing the rejecting? The text shows us. Earlier in Romans 11:12, the text reads, "Now if their transgression ...". Notice that the phrases "if their transgression" in verse 12 and "if their rejection" in verse 15 are parallel. In the Greek, the phrases are both in the same form, as they are in the English of the NASB and other English versions (NET, NRSV, NIV). Moreover they have the same idea. As "their transgression" meant the national repudiation of Messiah Yeshua, so does "their rejection" refer to that same repudiation of Messiah. Both phrases refer to Israel's national unbelief.

And what's the difference, you may ask? To translate the phrase "their being cast away" is to imply that God had cast away or rejected Israel for the time being. Many have adopted this very assumption. This would blatantly contradict Paul's argument of the chapter that "God has not rejected a people whom he foreknew" (Romans 11:1-2). We see that the point is precisely opposite. Though much of Israel has faithlessly rejected the Messiah, God is faithful and will not reject Israel! Therefore, just as Israel, and not God, did the transgressing, so also Israel, and not God, did the rejecting.

The reconciliation and salvation of lost people was always God's desire. If all Israel had been nationally saved when Yeshua first came, then the nation would have fulfilled their calling (in Exodus 19:6 as a "nation of priests") to preach Messiah to all nations. This national ministry will yet happen in the millennial Kingdom period (Isaiah 2:1-5; Micah 4:1-4). During this present time, because of the national rejection of Messiah, Paul and remnant Israel bring the Good News to all nations, representing Israel's national calling (2 Corinthians 5:18-20).

Also today, Jewish believers are the present representatives of Israel's national calling by their service. The Jewish believers' service might be directly to Israel, as was Peter's ministry, or it may be to the nations, as was Paul's ministry. The same is true for the remnant of the nations, Gentile believers. Wherever one is called, however, all are to have the same burden for Israel.

When Israel accepts (literally "takes" or "receives") Yeshua, that will mean "life from the dead" (Romans 11:15). Salvation is not thrust upon them, but offered, and they receive it. It is now and will always be by faith, trusting in what God has provided in Messiah.

"Life from the dead" may be thought to refer to Israel's redemption, that Israel is dead and will be made alive by acceptance of Yeshua. However, "life from the dead" is presented by Paul as a result of Israel being redeemed, not as equivalent to Israel being redeemed. Romans 11:15 is making a comparison: As Israel's rejection of Messiah resulted in "the reconciliation of the world," so their acceptance of Messiah will result in "life from the dead." It is for the world!

At first glance, "life from the dead" would certainly appear to include the resurrection of those who have died (as in Daniel 12:2; 1 Corinthians 15:20; Philippians 3:11). But this phrase entails even more: the restoration of the Kingdom. Worldwide revival, as in Isaiah 11:9, is a dead world made alive for God. When Yeshua establishes Messiah's kingdom on earth, it is the answer to the prayers, "Thy Kingdom come," and "come Lord Yeshua" (Matthew 6:10; Revelation 22:20). Since the redemption of Israel brings about this "life from the dead," one would think that those who pray "Thy Kingdom come" would be very active in sharing Yeshua with the Jewish people. Yes, the "dry bones" of Ezekiel 37:1-14 will live, and God's spirit will be put within them. And thus the Kingdom on earth as it is in heaven. The earth will be born again, even as Paul stated in Romans 8:17-22.

When God chose Abraham and his seed, He irrevocably chose them (Romans 11:29). Israel's present unbelief does not change that; Israel's faithlessness cannot nullify God's faithfulness (Romans 3:3). The resurrection and the Kingdom await Jewish revival when Israel receives Yeshua as King. Thus, all believers need to remember their calling. What about your activities? Your activities reflect your faith. Faithful Gentiles in Messiah reveal the faithfulness of God to Israel in Messiah. Godly living is extending the same grace which you received to others. Will you respond to your calling?

The Lord has made known His salvation;
He has revealed His righteousness in the
sight of the Nations.

Psalm 98:2

7

Their Own Olive Tree

One of the most misunderstood aspects of Romans 11 is the picture of the olive tree. Yet it is clear that the image is meant to bring Jews and Gentiles together in some sense. In this chapter we will examine the text and consider the meaning and significance of this enduring biblical symbol in Paul's letter.

The tree itself has some fascinating uses in Jewish history. Every part was used in service, especially Temple service. Its fruit could be used for food, oil, and salve; its wood was most favored for its beautiful appearance and durability (1 Kings 6:23-33); its leaves could be used for feeding livestock, its dried leaves for writing materials. Olive oil was used in the Temple for the anointing of all sacred articles, and to fuel the menorah. Even the olive pits were used for toothaches (Avodah Zarah 28). Thus, the tree itself came to symbolize Israel's service to God. The rabbis were pondering this symbolism even as late as the medieval era:

> For just as oil gives forth light, so did the Temple give light to the whole world, as it says, *and nations shall walk at thy light* (Isa. 60:3). Our forefathers were accordingly called "A leafy olive tree" because they gave light to all (with their faith) (Exodus Rabbah 36:1).

Yet Israel can be considered, not just this one plant, but many plants, an entire garden of God. In Zechariah 1:8 "the myrtle trees which were in the ravine" represent Israel in exile; the palm, cypress, cedar, and willows all had their meanings in context as well. In the New Covenant, we see three plants representing Israel and God's promises to them:

1. The vine symbolized Israel's spiritual life; this is Israel's productivity of promise. "For the vineyard of the Lord of hosts is the house of Israel" (Isaiah 5:1-7; Psalm 80:8-9; Hosea 10:1; and John 15:1-6).
2. The fig tree symbolized Israel's national life; this is Israel's profession of promise, "I saw your forefathers as the earliest fruit on the fig tree in its first season" (Hosea 9:10; Mark 11:12-14, 20; Matthew 24:32-34).
3. The olive tree symbolized Israel's ministerial life, Israel's privileges of promise. It spoke of Israel's calling and service: "The LORD called your name, 'A green olive tree, beautiful in fruit and form'" (Jeremiah 11:16; Hosea 14:6). In Romans 9:4-5, Paul writes of Israel,

> ...to whom belongs the adoption as sons and the glory and the covenants and the giving of the *torah* and the temple service and the promises, whose are the Fathers, and from whom is the Messiah according to the flesh, who is over all, God blessed forever. Amen.

Just as this passage connects God's promise to Israel with Israel's service to God, Paul uses the illustration of the olive tree to represent Israel's service. In a sense, these three plants picture for us three periods in Israel's history:

1. In the past, Israel was the vine, though pruned with the national rejection of the true Vine, Yeshua (John 15:1). The fruit of righteousness is only produced from abiding in Him. Though a remnant did abide in Messiah, by our national rejection of Messiah, the nation as a whole separated from the true Vine.

2. Israel in the present time is the fig tree. In Mark 11:13-14 Yeshua sought fruit from a fig tree, but it had no fruit, only leaves; so He cursed it. Israel as a nation has been withered, but only to the root (Mark 11:20). It was withered to represent God's displeasure with Israel's hypocrisy. Like the fig tree, we had the leaf (testimony) but not the fruit (substance). Despite Israel's religiosity, it was fruitless—God desires fruit, not mere religion.

3. Israel as the olive tree is a picture of our future service, when by faith in Messiah the natural branches are grafted back, "and thus all Israel will be saved" (Romans 11:26). In the millennial kingdom when Messiah reigns, Israel will once more be the head of nations (Deuteronomy 28:13, Micah 7:16-17), fulfilling their calling before God.

Thus in Romans 11:16-24, the olive tree also illustrates the ultimate goal of Gentile service: the national redemption of Israel. In his address to Gentile believers, Paul transitions from Romans 11:15 with a declaration of the impact of national Jewish revival in the coming kingdom, to verse 16, illustrating how that revival is inevitable. He uses two illustrations: first fruits' dough, and the root of an olive tree. Let us look at the first of these illustrations: "And if the first piece of dough is holy, the lump is also" (Romans 11:16). This dough is referring to Numbers 15:20-21:

> Of the first of your dough you shall lift up a cake as an offering; as the offering of the threshing floor, so you shall lift it up. From the first of your dough you shall give to the Lord an offering throughout your generations.

From the initial first fruits batch of dough would come the rest of the offering. If the first fruits are accepted, all the offerings to follow from that same batch would be accepted (Leviticus 23:10-12). Elsewhere, using this same principle, Paul assures the Corinthians that just as Yeshua was the first fruits from the dead, believers in Him will be resurrected as well

(1 Corinthians 15:20-23). As the first fruits are, so also is the batch.

Here, the patriarchs, or more specifically, the promises made to the patriarchs, are the first fruits. Thus Paul wrote in Romans 11:28, "they [Israel] are beloved for the sake of *the fathers.*" Again, he would later write in Romans 15:8, "Messiah has become a servant to the circumcision [Israel] on behalf of the truth of God *to confirm the promises given to the fathers.*"

By faith the fathers were first fruits, and as such were holy, that is, set apart unto the Lord. Also, their offspring, Israel, had a holy position as Moses noted: "For you are a holy people to the LORD your God" (Deuteronomy 7:6). Thus, Paul continued "if the root is holy, so are the branches." The tree is Israel, and the root is the promises made to the fathers. Paul changed metaphors, from a lump of dough to a tree, but the idea is the essentially the same. In this, we see the principle that "whatever touches them shall be holy" (Exodus 30:29, Leviticus 6:18).

WILD BRANCHES GRAFTED IN TO SERVE

From that *principle* of the root Paul proceeds to describe the *partaking* of the root:

> But if some of the branches were broken off, and you, being a wild olive, were grafted in among them and became partaker with them of the rich root of the olive tree. (Romans 11:17)

Paul says to the Gentile believers, "and you, being a wild olive, were grafted in among them." Note that it is not *instead of* them, but *among* them. Gentile believers, as wild olive branches, are added to the olive tree among the natural believing branches. Gentiles do not replace Jewish people.

Partaking of the root means depending on the promises of God, which provide the spiritual nourishment for the soul. It is possible to be saved, but under-nourished: feeding on fear, anxiety, or pride, and not on His promises by faith. We are to "desire the pure milk of the Word that you may grow in respect to salvation" (1 Peter 2:2), and to "seek first the Kingdom of God and His righteousness and all these things will be added on to you" (Matthew 6:33).

This idea of grafting Gentiles into Israel is understood in traditional Judaism:

> "R. Eleazar further stated: What is meant by the text, and in thee shall the families of the earth be blessed? The Holy One, blessed be He, said to Abraham, 'I have two goodly shoots to engraft on you: Ruth the Moabitess and Naamah the Ammonitess'. (Both belonged to idolatrous nations and were 'grafted' upon the stock of Israel. The former was the ancestress of David (Ruth 4:13 ff), and the latter the mother of Rehoboam (1 Kings 14:31) and his distinguished descendants Asa, Jehoshaphat and Hezekiah.)" (Yevamot 63a; cf. Leviticus Rabbah 1:2)

One view of the olive tree is that it represents salvation; thus being "broken off" means "to forfeit one's salvation." However, in the text and in the larger context, the olive tree does not refer to Israel's salvation (in the body of Messiah), but to Israel's service. So also, to be broken off is to be removed from that service. This is an important distinction. Because of his arrogance and disobedience, Samson was blinded and removed from service for the Lord, and ended up serving the pagans. Yet, the New Covenant names this same Samson among the heroes of faith (Hebrews 11:32)! Removal from service does not mean a loss of salvation, though in the case of the natural branches that were broken off, they are without salvation apart from Messiah. Those who believe will receive, along with salvation, a return to service in the Lord. When Paul says to the wild branches, "nor will He spare you," Gentiles are threatened with being likewise broken off. This refers also to their removal from service.

Though God is not a respecter of persons (Romans 2:11), He is a respecter of positions that He has established. Jewish people are set apart by the root into a place of calling, and if they will believe, into a place of blessing. The calling is holy, and should be respected even if the individual is unworthy (see Acts 23:5). This is why David was careful to do nothing to despise King Saul in his position, though Saul was unworthy and didn't live up to that position (1 Samuel 24 and 26). This is why we are to honor our fathers and mothers, though they may not live up to their calling as parents.

The position may be holy, but the individual in the position is blessed and saved only by personally depending on the Lord, not by having a position. So regardless of anyone's position: "without faith it is impossible to please Him" (Hebrews 11:6). In any case, as the promises to Abraham are certain, so we are certain that God will restore Israel when they come to faith in Yeshua. This certainty in God's promises is seen in one's attitude toward Jewish people, the natural branches.

Regarding the removal of Jewish people from service, only "some of the branches were broken off," not all of them. As we have studied, Israel's unbelief is only partial. Only the unbelieving, natural branches—as many as that may be—are broken off from service. Was God through with Israel during Elijah's day, or in the wilderness with Moses? No, He was not. As a witness nation, Israel lives on through the remnant of believing natural branches.

There is a holy call upon the Jewish people to serve God, and the fulfillment of that call comes by faith. Jewish people individually respond with faith in Yeshua in order to enjoy the blessings and service that accompany salvation. Faith sets you apart; unbelief sets you aside.

IGNORANCE LEADS TO ARROGANCE

As the Roman believers went from the principle of the root (16), to partaking of the root (17), now in verse 18, Paul teaches them to understand the 'pillar' of the root. As a pillar supports a building, Gentiles are supported by the promises of

God. Therefore Paul warns them, "do not be arrogant toward the branches; but if you are arrogant, remember that it is not you who supports the root, but the root supports you." Jewish believers and unsaved Jewish people are all natural branches. Therefore, the phrase "do not be arrogant towards the branches" means do not be arrogant toward the Jewish people, neither toward Jewish believers who are "in the tree" and in service, nor toward unsaved Jewish people who have been "broken off."

Arrogance towards the natural branches is, sadly, a part of the history of the church. This arrogance toward the natural branches is seen in anti-Semitism. This anti-Semitism can be theological, where people are taught that God is through with the Jewish people or that the Church has replaced Israel. It can also be as subtle as telling a Jewish believer that it is inappropriate to maintain one's Jewishness after coming to faith in Yeshua. The arrogance is so ingrained in most church teaching that all of the feasts are written off as merely 'Jewish traditions', even though as pointers to Messiah they were observed by the Messiah Himself, His apostles, and the first century believers (Luke 22:7-8; Acts 20:6, 16).

Some may think of the Jewish people as the people who keep the Scriptures. But the truth of matter is: It is not the people that keep the Book, but the Book that keeps the people! Though we could not keep the precepts of *torah*, the promises of *torah* can keep us (Acts 15:10)! The same root upholds both Jews and Gentiles who depend upon it.

> You will say then, "Branches were broken off so that I might be grafted in." (Romans 11:19)

In the text, "I" (*ego*) is emphasized. Once after a rabbi preached a sermon on pride, a woman wanted to speak with him. "Rabbi," she said, "I am in much distress of mind. I need to confess to a great sin." The rabbi asked her, "What is this great sin?" "Oh," she answered, "the sin of pride. Some days I sit before my mirror for hours admiring my exquisite beauty."

"Hmm," responded the rabbi, "that was not a sin of pride—that was a sin of hallucination."

Arrogance blinds us to our actual condition, and substitutes it with a superior attitude about self. Some Gentile believers might even think that "God removed certain natural branches in order to make room for us." The arrogant branches can act as if God is saying, "Wow, the Gentiles are available as branches! Great, get rid of the Jews"; or as if God is a new car salesman, "Got to get rid of the 2010 models to make room for the 2011 models!" Yes, branches were broken off for their unbelief, but that doesn't mean you're any better!

> Quite right, they were broken off for their unbelief, but you stand by your faith. Do not be conceited, but fear; for if God did not spare the natural branches, neither will He spare you. (Romans 11:20-21)

Just as broken off branches were removed for faithlessness, it is only by faith that we ourselves remain—that is, if we respond with reverential fear. What has happened to national Israel, their temporary loss of service, can happen to Gentile believers as well: they too can be removed from service.

In a sense, arrogance actually produces insecurity, because only God's promise, not our abilities or genetics, can secure us. Some may have prayed sincerely, been able to trace their ancestry back to Sinai, kept all the feasts, strived to be righteous, and known the intricacies of the Hebrew text. Yet, without faith in Messiah, they have been broken off. Thus, without faith, God will not keep you in service either. Any of us can go "from hero to zero" in an instant. "Pride goes before destruction, and a haughty spirit before a fall" (Proverbs 16:18).

KINDNESS AND SEVERITY

Without appreciation for the natural branches, we do not appreciate the root that produced the branches. Looking down on the broken off branches can only mean that you're not looking up to the One who is seated at the right hand of the

Father. Arrogance toward the Jews is arrogance toward God's promises which He made to the Fathers.

This can be remedied through reverence and reliance on Messiah, which will reveal a compassion and concern for the Jewish people.

In Romans 11:22-24, Paul then teaches that this arrogance is belittling to His kindness (v. 22), His power (v. 23), and His provision (v. 24). In verse 22, arrogance belittles God's kindness: He can remove Gentiles as easily as He broke off the natural branches:

> Behold then the kindness and severity of God; to those who fell, severity, but to you, God's kindness, if you continue in His kindness; otherwise you also will be cut off.

Gentile believers are not to take His kindness lightly (Romans 2:4). His kindness expresses "the riches of His grace" (Ephesians 2:7). All that God has done for us in salvation, and all that He enables us to do in service for Him, is by His kindness. But, we must continue by faith, or be cut off from service by our own faithlessness.

The cure for conceit is the fear of chastening from a holy God. If need be, God can remove us from service for a time. By such discipline we can then receive humility by faith, and humility that follows chastening can again restore us for service. Seeing others removed is a reminder to revere the Lord.

RELYING ON THE LORD'S POWER

Gentile believers must not forget how they have been enabled to serve. Paul therefore writes, "And they also, if they do not continue in their unbelief, will be grafted in, for God is able to graft them in again" (Romans 11:23). Arrogance is reflected in the fact that some think that God's promises to Jewish people are now voided or transferred. This belittles His power. Through God's promise and His power, He is able to graft them in again. His promises remain, and the Jewish people need only to trust in Yeshua to enjoy those promises.

The same power that saved lost Gentiles will save the lost sheep of the house of Israel, for it is the same faith that saved Gentiles that will save Jewish people as well.

It's a little like a father saying to his son who was caught driving too fast: "the car is still yours, but until you repent, you're grounded." The promises still belong to Israel, but they can only enjoy them through a restored relationship to their God, through repentance and faith.

How is this possible after the national rejection of Messiah? Can God bring Israel back to the same land after 19 centuries? Yes, He can. God can give 90 year-old Sarah a baby, feed more than 5,000 with five loaves and two little fish, and even raise the dead. God is able! This is the theme of Scripture, and the theme of every life that trusts in the Lord. He can even save you, and deliver you.

From time to time, spiritual leaders are exposed for moral failure, and are rightly removed from service. The world may laugh and call them hypocrites, which is true, but each of us are susceptible to temptation. However, some have then repented of their sin and even false teaching, and are restored to service and honor. Failure need not be the last word on anyone's life.

In the future Millennial reign of Messiah, Israel will once more nationally be grafted back in, and will be the head of nations in service for the Lord (see Deuteronomy 28:13; Micah 7:16-17). The same God who keeps you by His promise and power will one day restore Israel to her promised place, for His word is true and He is able!

Arrogance toward the natural branches not only forgets God's power, but also belittles His provision to the Gentile branches:

> For if you were cut off from what is by nature a wild olive tree, and were grafted contrary to nature into a cultivated olive tree, how much more will these who are the natural branches be grafted into their own olive tree? (Romans 11:24)

Gentile believers are "contrary to nature." What does that mean? Normally a cultivated graft is placed into a wild tree to attain its vigor, and to produce cultivated fruit. But God took wild fruitless branches and grafted them into the cultivated tree. God worked contrary to nature, yet the wild olive branch now bears fruit. Like a square peg in a round hole, God took what cannot work naturally and by grace made it work.

By His grace, God has brought Gentiles to believe in His Jewish Messiah, His Jewish prophets, His Jewish apostles, His Jewish Scriptures. He grafted them into a Jewish hope! The "cultivated olive tree," into which Gentile believers have been grafted, representing the Jewish civilization up until that point. This tree was cultivated over many generations of God's work through Abraham, Moses, and the prophets. You have not entered a wild and unexplored territory which needs to be tamed. This is not an unfurnished home that needs your special touch. Rather, identifying with biblically Jewish faith is for Gentiles "contrary to nature." It may be uncomfortable to you at first, and may take some getting used to. The problem is that when Gentiles began to outnumber the natural branches, especially in leadership, they began to change things to make it feel more comfortable.

The Jewish people are still the natural branches, and thus they fit into "their own olive tree." If God can save Gentiles by bringing them into what is contrary by nature, then how much more can He save Jews through what is familiar to Jewish people!

In a sense, the Gentiles are supposed to be the 'hard work', since it is not part of their background, and Jewish work should be comparatively easy. After all, Messiah is the goal of *torah* (Romans 10:4). The olive tree service *still* belongs to the Jewish people; it never became wild, Gentile, or non-Jewish. Israel should be able to recognize the Good News through the witness of Gentile believers, since that message represents their original calling of service to the God of Israel.

The point is not that diverse cultures should be obliterated in favor of one uniform Jewish culture. Not at all: may every tribe and tongue profess His Name! However, if Yeshua is not presented as Israel's Messiah, He has no qualifications to be anyone's Savior. This loss of His identity to Israel is due not primarily to Israel's rejection, but to Gentile arrogance. Its not for those who rejected Messiah to represent Him faithfully, but those who received Him. Embracing the calling to make Israel jealous entails a gracious recognition that service to Yeshua is "their own olive tree."

As already argued, Messianic congregations are necessary. However, Messiah's body is one, and not to be divided into wings, sections, or camps. So the considerations involved in our service do not merely affect merely one part, but the whole. Yes, the Jewish people know that churches exist. Still, in a sense, the vast majority of churches which honor Jesus are invisible to my people, and its mainly due to a disguise. If a church intends to carry out its service and worship explicitly for the God of Israel, why is this reality kept hidden from the Jewish people?

As a young believer, I was asked to debate with a rabbi about whether Jesus is the Messiah. Set up by the Jewish women's organization Hadassah, the debate was held in the basement of a Lutheran church. I gave my testimony, and throughout the night, we went back and forth about the Messiah.

There were several other rabbis in the audience. One asked how I could believe Yeshua was God, and he became especially offended as I then quoted Isaiah 9:5 in Hebrew. Eventually, it got so heated that they had to stop the debate. "Come with me; I want to talk to you," the rabbi said, taking me and a few other Jewish believers upstairs to the sanctuary. There were pictures of Jesus and Mary, crosses and stained glass everywhere. "Rabbi," I said, with all sincerity, "we really believe that Jesus is the Messiah."

The rabbi was livid as he looked around the room, taking in the environment. Pointing at the symbols, he was aghast. "This?" he pleaded, "this is what you are worshiping?"

There are no simple solutions; its much easier to turn around a small dinghy than a big ship. Yet, we must face the reality that instead of identifying with the Jewish Messiah, and having a Jewish frame of reference, much of the body of Messiah has over time come to adapt to an expression of faith which is more comfortable for their majority.

Suppose I take a trip to Israel, and my assistant Pat uses my office while I am away. Yet, looking around, he does not feel at home there. The pictures of my family are not his family, so he changes that. The paint color also is not to his taste, so it has to go. The door on that left wall is not where he would want it, and so he changes it to the other wall. Actually, the location of the office itself is not convenient for him, so he moves the office to a space on his side of town. When I finally return, I cannot even find my office, let alone recognize it. How did that happen? Its simple: He acted like I was not coming back!

Gentiles have acted like Jewish people would never return. Well, by God's grace many of us are back and will continue coming back—and we may not fully appreciate what you have done with the place! Have our congregations and communities prized comfort and familiarity over the Good News? It is never too late to repent, so that the testimony of Messiah will be furthered in Israel!

On your walls, O Jerusalem, I have appointed watchmen; all day and all night. You, who remind the Lord, take no rest for yourselves; and give Him no rest until He establishes and makes Jerusalem a praise in the earth.

Isaiah 62:6-7

8

The Fullness of the Gentiles

> "For I do not want you, brethren, to be uninformed of this mystery – so that you will not be wise in your own estimation – that a partial hardening has happened to Israel until the fullness of the Gentiles has come in."
> (Romans 11:25)

We have considered Romans 11:11-24, seeing how the Gentiles have been redeemed so as to provoke Israel to jealousy. Then we considered how in the olive tree, Gentiles are grafted into the service of Israel, and thus should not be arrogant to the natural branches, nor should they presume to "Gentilize" the service into which they have been grafted. In Romans 11:25-32, Paul concludes his teaching on God's faithfulness to Israel.

Israel's present rejection of Messiah and their future restoration was a mystery to the Gentile believers in Rome. This mystery of Israel included: the purpose of Israel's stumbling, their position of service, and the promise of their salvation. In this chapter, we will take an in-depth look at Romans 11:25-32 and the promise of salvation.

109

THE MYSTERY OF ISRAEL'S PROMISED REDEMPTION

Gentile believers who are wise in their own eyes are those who boast against the natural branches, trusting in themselves. When Paul says, "For I do not want you, brethren, to be uninformed of this mystery – so that you will not be wise in your own estimation," he implies that there is a need to understand this mystery. Ignorance can lead to arrogance. Like all good leaders, Paul does not want his disciples to be ignorant, but rather to be living in the truth of God's will. If only all leaders shared his desire! At any rate, some believers of Paul's day were uninformed, as their attitudes revealed.

The word "mystery" (*musterion* in the Greek) is something formerly unknown but now revealed (Romans 16:25; Ephesians 1:9-10; 3:4-9; 5:32; Colossians 1:26-27; 2:2; 4:3; 2 Thessalonians 2:7; 1 Timothy 3:9; 3:16; Revelation 1:20).[1] In other words, Paul is explaining a mystery, not creating one. Its not a mystery merely about a future chronology, but about relating to their present ministry.

Hardness has happened to Israel, but only in part (Romans 11:25). Paul reiterates that there is an unbelieving part of Israel alongside the believing remnant (Romans 11:5). They are physical Israel, or Paul's "kinsmen according to the flesh," though the remnant is spiritual Israel (Romans 9:3, 6). But this situation is temporary:

> Until the fullness of the Gentiles comes in, and thus all Israel will be saved. (Romans 11:25-26)

Opinions differ regarding the meaning of this phrase, "until the fullness of the Gentiles comes in" (Romans 11:25). In what follows, I will be parsing and considering the phrase itself (pp 111-114), as well as evaluating various views regarding its meaning (pp 114-119). My own position is found on page 117, number 5.

---

1   Barclay-Newman Greek English Dictionary; Gingrich Greek NT Lexicon

There are several considerations to determine the meaning of this phrase:
1. Purpose - to keep Gentiles from conceit.
2. Context - the themes of the chapter.
3. Audience - the Gentile believers Paul was addressing.
4. Meaning - accounting for the language used:
   - "until"
   - "fullness"
   - "the fullness of the Gentiles."
   - "comes in" (one word in Greek)
   - "and thus"

1) Purpose was to keep Gentiles from conceit

Some believe that in this present age God is not working with Israel. The idea is that the Jewish people have been blinded so that God might now work among the Gentiles. There are others as well who state that God is completely finished with the Jews as a people, and that "the Church" is now Israel. These are examples of the very arrogance that Paul is concerned with in this section. Paul is trying to show that God is working among Israel even in the present time. The Gentile branches have not replaced Israel at all, but are grafted in among them (11:17-18). The revelation of the mystery of Israel was to help Gentile believers see God's purpose for their lives, as well as to protect them from becoming arrogant (Romans 11:25).

2) The context of the chapter

The phrase "the fullness of the Gentiles" must fit into the context of what Paul has already taught. First, even though Israel has nationally rejected the Messiah, God has not rejected

Israel (Romans 11:1-2, 15). Second, the national Jewish rejection of Messiah has resulted in partial, temporary removal from divine service.

Third, in light of this rejection, the Good News came to the Gentiles in order to make Israel jealous (Romans 11: 11). This desire to make them jealous is exemplified by Paul's willingness to do anything to reach his own Jewish people, even though he was the Apostle to the Gentiles (Romans 11:13-14). Thus his work in evangelizing the Gentiles is strategic: Gentile believers play a vital part in God's work to reach and redeem Israel.

3) Practical and applicable for the Gentile audience

The Gentile Great Commission is to provoke Israel to desire a relationship with the God of Israel through faith in Yeshua. Through sensitivity and cultural relevance, merciful Gentiles make Israel jealous. Believers live in such a way that Jewish communities can understand the message of Israel's Messiah. An example of this is Luke. Though according to most scholars he was a Gentile, he was discipled by Paul and understood and communicated the faith in a biblically Jewish frame of reference (Acts 20:6).

Paul only uses "the fullness of the Gentiles" in this section, in light of his instruction to the Gentiles concerning God's faithfulness to Israel. Naturally, it would have been of little concern for some Gentiles that there is a future hope for the Jewish people: "That's nice for Israel, but what about me?" Paul's teaching had to offer some practical, as well as theological help to the Gentiles in their present spiritual walk.

4) Meaning of the language used

- **"Until"** – The partial hardening has happened to Israel "until the fullness of the Gentiles has come in." The word "until" signifies that there is an assured end of the hardness for national Israel.

- **"Fullness"** in the Greek is *pleroma* (from *playro'o* "to fill"). Some translate this word as "full number" here (NIV, NRSV). However, *pleroma* is never translated this way elsewhere, but rather as "fullness" or "fulfillment" as in Romans 11:12. If the emphasis on number or quantity was to be Paul's point, there are other Greek words he could have used. In the Septuagint (LXX), the Greek word for fixed "number" is *arithmou* (we get the word "arithmetic" from it). This is used for an exact number as in Revelation 7:4, "the number [*arithmon*] of those who were sealed, one hundred and forty-four thousand," and also for very large quantities (Revelation 20:8). Paul would have used this word if there were a fixed number of Gentiles intended by the term. However, the word *pleroma*, which he uses in this verse, does not deal with numbers. Rather, it refers to a quality of fulfillment:

  For of His fullness we have all received, and grace upon grace. (John 1:16)

  The earth is the Lord's, and all its fullness. (1 Corinthians 10:26)

  For in Him all the fullness of Deity dwells in bodily form. (Colossians 2:9)

- **"The fullness of the Gentiles"** – as mentioned, *pleroma* is also used in Romans 11:12: "Now if their transgression is riches for the world and their failure is riches for the Gentiles, how much more will their fulfillment (*pleroma*) be." Israel's fullness is contrasted with their national "transgression" and "failure," not to a number (such as the remnant of Israel). Israel's fullness or fulfillment is tied to their national response to the Good News.

The promised fullness for Israel is when they fulfill their calling to bless the nations, which will mean life from the dead (Romans 11:15). Likewise, Gentile believers' obedience is their fulfillment. Obedience to what? The mandate of Romans

11:11, which is reiterated in the following verses: the very same mercy that Gentiles received by grace through Israel's Messiah, they are to minister back to Israel in their national disobedience (Romans 11:30-31). Gentile fulfillment is for Israel's benefit.

- **"Comes in"** – The verb "come in" (*eiselthe*) certainly need not imply a number of individuals coming in, as we see the word used when "sin entered (*eiselthen*) into the world" (Romans 5:12). Just as sin "entered into" the world and brought death, the obedience of Gentiles by "coming into" their ministry to the Jewish people will bring life, mercy, and salvation. This "entering in" of the Gentiles contrasts with failing to entering into the fullness of ministry due to unbelief (Hebrews 3:19; 4:6-11).

- **"And thus"** – This phrase connects "the fullness of the Gentiles come in," with "all Israel will be saved," indicating a logical result. Even though Israel was partially hardened, nevertheless they will be fully saved. Israel's salvation is a direct result of the fullness of the Gentiles.

EVALUATION

With this criteria in hand, there are several options to consider regarding this phrase, "the fullness of the Gentiles."

1. The glory of the Church – A popular view is that "the fullness of the Gentiles" refers to the glory of the Church. Those who interpret the phrase in this manner see the Church as a replacement for Israel. This interpretation explains the connection to "all Israel will be saved," by claiming that "the fullness of the Gentiles" simply *is* "all Israel."

However, this view is contrary to the context of the chapter, where Israel is clearly distinct from the Gentiles. In Romans 11:25, Israel is blind in part, and in 11:26, Israel is equated with Jacob. Those who are blind in part in Romans 11:25 are the same as all Israel who are saved in Romans 11:26. Clearly,

Israel is spoken of as needing redemption. Does it make sense to assume the believing church is Israel here, that the believing church remains in blind unbelief?

The mystery that Paul is explaining is not regarding the fullness of salvation of the Gentiles, but of Israel. It is not that Israel is blinded so that the fullness of the Gentiles can come in (Romans 11:12), but the fullness of the Gentiles leads to an end of Israel's blindness.

2. The full number of Gentiles saved – Another popular view is that "the fullness of the Gentiles" refers to when Gentile multitudes will be gathered in as a last-days harvest. This view is held by many of our evangelical brethren, particularly premillennial dispensationalists who hold to a pre-tribulation rapture of the body of Messiah (1 Thessalonians 4:16-5:5).

The idea here is that when God saves an elected number of Gentiles, He then will begin working with Israel. When the last Gentile is saved, then the rapture will take place, and God will turn to the Jewish people. In the extreme end of this view, some people reason that reaching out to Gentiles (and not Jews) is the only way to help Israel, since every Gentile who is reached means we are that much closer to the time when God will again work with Israel.

This view has several difficulties. *First,* the term "fullness" should not be thought of as a number or quantity, as this view assumes.

Second, though it is proper to make a distinction between Israel and the Body of Messiah (a body of Jewish and Gentile believers), this view is dependent on the premise of a Gentile Church without Jewish believers. In reality, in this present age, the Good News is to the Jew first, not last. The Rapture can no more be tied to the fullness of the Gentiles than it can be called the fullness of the Jews.

115

Third, multitudes of Gentiles will be saved during the Tribulation. In fact, Romans 11:12 and 15 makes it clear that only after all Israel is saved will the greater blessings come to Gentiles. To identify the fullness of the Gentiles with the last Gentile being saved does not work. For all we know, the last person saved before the Rapture might actually be a Jewish person!

The notion that God is primarily working among the Gentiles as opposed to Israel is taken from Acts 15:14-18. In this section, Jacob (James) recognizes that it was always God's intention to save Gentiles along with Israel. Yet nothing in the passage suggests that God was through working with the Jewish people in this present age.

3. The judgment on the Gentile unbelievers – There is another view that "the fullness of the Gentiles" refers to judgment on the Gentiles, or "the times of the Gentiles" (Luke 21:24). Commendably, this would keep the Gentiles from conceit in line with the purpose of the chapter. However, this view seems to create more problems than it solves. The word "fullness" would have an opposite meaning in Romans 11:25 as the same word has in 11:12. The issue of judgment on the Gentiles does not fit into the context. Paul is teaching Gentile believers to minister, not assuring them of future judgment.

4. The return of exiled Israelites from among the Nations – The Hebrew phrase *m'lo-hagoyim* ("multitude of nations," Genesis 48:19), though not translated from the Hebrew as "fullness of the Gentiles" in most English translations, can mean this in other contexts (including Hebrew translations of Romans 11:25, following Delitzsch). Some Messianic believers have drawn a connection between the two passages, such that Paul envisioned the phrase to refer to Jews coming in from among the Gentile nations (Ezekiel 37:1-14). Also a similar "Two-House" interpretation has surfaced which refers the fullness of

Romans 11:25 to Ephraimites returning and reuniting with the house of Judah.

The errors of Two-House theory go beyond our focus, as it rests upon a forced distinction within Israel (see chapter 12); it has also been considered in sufficient depth by others. But as for "fullness of the Gentiles" referring to Israel's return from exile, while I love the idea of having Paul speak to that hope, the language does not permit this interpretation. The Hebrew words coincide, but the Greek in Romans 11:25 is different than the Septuagint for Genesis 48:19. Whereas the Greek in Genesis 48:19 means "multitude" (*plethos*), the word used in Romans certainly does not. Moreover, the preceding context for the term he does use (*pluroma*) goes against such a connection in every respect (Romans 11:12). Besides all this, the context of Genesis 48:19 probably does not speak of Israel becoming a multitude in exile. Rather, as Rashi notes, it more likely refers to Joshua leading Israel in conquering the nations, though it may have an application of influence among the nations (ibn Ezra).

5. The faithfulness of the Gentile believers – I (and others) see "fullness of the Gentiles" as referring to the faithfulness of Gentile believers obediently ministering to Israel. This fits the context, would be understandable and applicable to Gentile readers, and would be in line with Paul's motivation of keeping the Gentiles from conceit.

In Romans 11:12 the word fullness has to do with the completion of Israel's ministry; they will be faithful in obedience to Messiah and fulfill their calling. In Romans 11:25 this same word refers to Gentiles completing their own ministry, to faithfully do God's will in making Israel jealous. This leads to all Israel being saved. The fullness of the Gentiles therefore means God's completion of His work among the Gentiles as it relates to Israel.

We are not saved by works, but works reflect on our spiritual maturity. The fullness of maturity for the Gentile believer is directly tied to Jewish ministry. Just as immaturity hides the Good News, so maturity reveals the Good News. It is immaturity not to help others, especially those by whom you have been helped. Gentile fulfillment is for Israel's benefit, and your fulfillment is found in ministering to others.

This is the fulfillment of the hope written in the Prophets, that the nations (Gentiles) will be a blessing to Israel.

> And many nations will join themselves to the LORD in that day and will become My people. Then I will dwell in your midst, and you will know that the LORD of hosts has sent Me to you. (Zechariah 2:11)

> Thus says the Lord GOD, "Behold, I will lift up My hand to the nations, and set up My standard to the peoples; and they will bring your sons in their bosom, and your daughters will be carried on their shoulders." (Isaiah 49:22)

> For thus says the LORD, "Behold, I extend peace to her like a river, and the glory of the nations like an overflowing stream; and you shall be nursed, you shall be carried on the hip and bounced on the knees." (Isaiah 66:12)

Therefore, fullness for Gentile believers is their faithfulness to enter into a ministry of service to Israel. The point is not to fill up the "Gentile church," but to restore this Jewish olive tree, for the benefit of all.

> And so all Israel will be saved; just as it is written, "The Deliverer will come from Zion, He will remove ungodliness from Jacob. This is My covenant with them, when I take away their sins." (Romans 11:26-27)

Israel will be restored nationally according to God's permanent promises. "All Israel" pictures a collective, national turning to Messiah, but there are still lost individual Jewish people. Likewise, our sages taught, "All Israel shall have a share in the world to come." Yet the portion then lists those within

Israel who will not have a share in the world to come, which includes among other things, those who deny the resurrection (Mishnah, Sanhedrin 10:1).

As a result of the fulfilled Gentile ministry "all Israel will be saved." Our reason for this assurance is "just as it is written." He references Isaiah 59:20-21 and 27:9 to show that God has always desired all Israel to be saved. So why is Paul saying this to Gentiles? Because it is specifically their fullness which is achieved, as they live faithfully in light of God's promises.

THE SALVATION PROBLEM IS INTERNAL

Deliverance is a spiritual issue, not a political one: the Deliverer will "remove ungodliness and take away their sins." In Paul's day, Israel's real problem was not the Romans, but personal sin. In our day, the real problem is not Hamas, Iran, or the economy: the problem is still ungodliness.

In the first century many Israelites rejected Yeshua because they thought their problem was external: the Romans. Yeshua, however, taught that the issue was internal. Their sin separated them from God: "I said therefore to you, that you shall die in your sins; for unless you believe that I am, you shall die in your sins" (John 8:24; 10:23-25; Isaiah 59:1-2). It is the same with each of us: the problem is not external circumstances, but internal sin.

Although our need for salvation is internal, the provision for salvation is external. Though Isaiah 59:20-21 refers to God redeeming Israel, the rabbis applied it to Messiah as Israel's Redeemer (Sanhedrin 98a). Your redemption and salvation will not be from what you can do for yourself, but from beyond yourself, from another—the Deliverer. In the story of Ruth we see the idea of a "kinsman redeemer," in this case Boaz, who paid the price to redeem Ruth from widowhood. In Hebrew, a *goel* is a kinsman-redeemer who delivers his kin from capture and death.

"And a Redeemer will come to Zion, and to those who turn from transgression in Jacob," declares the Lord. "And as for Me, this is My covenant with them...through this Jacob's iniquity will be forgiven" (Isaiah 59:20-21; 27:9).

The kinsman redeemer had to be a family member, yet the Scripture says that God is our Redeemer. In the incarnation of Messiah, God became family to redeem us. Yeshua is Israel's *goel*, their Kinsman Redeemer.

There are three deliverances by Yeshua in the Scriptures:

1. All believers today are delivered from the domain of darkness (Colossians 1:13; Matthew 6:13; 2 Timothy 3:11; 4:18)
2. All believers will be delivered from the Tribulation to come (1 Thessalonians 1:10; 2 Peter 3:9)
3. All Israel will be delivered from the destruction of the enemy (Romans 11:26)

Israel nationally rejected Messiah. This is a mystery illustrated throughout the Scriptures. For instance, in Genesis, Joseph was rejected by his brethren, but was later revealed to them as their savior. Like Joseph, Yeshua will finally be revealed to the Jewish people as their Savior. Moses was initially rejected by Israel, but at his return he became their deliverer.

In the same manner at His return, Yeshua will be accepted as Deliverer of Israel. The relationship for Israel nationally—or for you individually—is based upon forgiveness of sins that Messiah brings: there can be no relationship with God without first the removal of sin (1 John 1:7, 9).

Messiah delivered us from sin's penalty, He can deliver us from sin's power, and will one day deliver us from sin's presence! He sets us free to follow Him home.

THE PLACE OF REDEMPTION

Interestingly, Isaiah 59:20-21 says "to Zion," but here Romans 11:26 says "from Zion." Why the difference? In the Scriptures, Zion is Jerusalem (2 Samuel 5:7; Psalm 51:18; Isaiah 2:3). The difference could be that the Scriptures are reiterating the fact that Israel's future redeemer will be a Jew, coming "out from Zion." But more likely, it refers to the Zion above, the heavenly Zion, of which the earthly Zion is merely a reminder: "you have come to Mount Zion and to the city of the living God, the heavenly Jerusalem" (Hebrews 12:22; Galatians 4:26; Revelation 3:12).

Paul is looking ahead to the Second Coming of Messiah, when Yeshua returns directly from Heaven as Kinsman Redeemer to save the Jewish people. So we await our present blessed hope, "for His Son from Heaven, whom He raised from the dead, that is Yeshua, who rescues us from the wrath to come" (1 Thessalonians 1:10).

THE PARDON FOR REDEMPTION

When Messiah returns, the New Covenant will then be applied to Israel.

> In that day a fountain will be opened for the house of David and for the inhabitants of Jerusalem, for sin and for impurity. (Zechariah 13:1)

Following this cleansing from sin, national Israel enters into a new relationship with God, just like all believers do, which is detailed in the New Covenant (Jeremiah 31:31-34). Don't let the present partial hardness distract you from the promised national wholeness.

Our lives are oriented around His promises, not our problems. Israel's and your present problems will eventually be removed, but God's promises will remain.

ISRAEL'S POSITION OF SERVICE

> From the standpoint of the Good News they are enemies for your sake, but from the standpoint of God's choice they are beloved for the sake of the fathers; for the gifts and the calling of God are irrevocable. (Romans 11:28-29)

Paradoxically, the majority of the natural branches are broken off from service for their unbelief. Therefore they are enemies of the Good News. Yet they are beloved? Paul teaches us how we are to treat Israel in light of this apparent contradiction. In the short-term, unbelieving Jewish people are enemies of the gospel. Before anyone comes to believe in Yeshua, indeed, "while we were enemies, we were reconciled to God through the death of His Son" (Romans 5:10). As "enemies," all people are under the wrath of God until they place their faith in and receive Yeshua as their Savior (Romans 1:18).

In the long-term, unbelieving Jewish people are beloved by God for the fathers' sake. The enemy status of the majority of Israel is a short-term perspective, but their beloved status is a long-term (eternal) perspective. Is your perspective on the Jewish people long-term or short-term? We can sometimes be pretty tough on others, even ourselves. In your recent failures you can judge yourself as a loser, even an enemy. But in the long-term, because of God's promises, you are beloved. God hasn't given up on you.

That's why Paul says, "For your sake," that is, for your advantage, the Good News came to the Gentiles. It is like a football game, where the star quarterback had to be pulled out of the game for not listening to the coach. The coach then replaced the experienced quarterback with a rookie, to show that with the coach's game plan anyone can win, if they will only trust the coach and follow his plan. Paul calls Israel, "my brethren according to the flesh ... to whom belongs the adoption as sons, and the glory and the covenants and the giving of the

Law and the temple service and the promises" (Romans 9:3b-4). If Israel is presently sidelined and Gentiles, 'the rookie' have been put into the game to follow the Coach's plan. Therefore, don't get arrogant and change the plan, rookie, or you might get benched too. Stay with the game plan.

God sovereignly loves Israel for the fathers' sake, that is, they are beloved by reason of the promises given to the fathers. You experience that love by faith in Messiah. Jewish people are not hated by God but are loved by God –and by those whom the love of Messiah fills. You serve them not for the way they are towards you, but for the way God is towards them.

> For the gifts and the calling of God are irrevocable. (Romans 11: 29)

God's character gives a long-range perspective on the problem. The use of Israel's gifts (detailed out in Romans 9:4-5) and the fulfillment of their national calling may be sidelined for now, but not forever. The calling belongs to Israel, but without faith it is unusable. Why are we still beloved? Because there is no repentance with God.

Making "the Church" Israel renders the existence of the Jewish people as a national entity a matter of indifference to the God of Israel. Israel's position of service is permanently irrevocable because the promises of God are irrevocable. Scripture says of Israel, "to whom belongs the adoption as sons" (Romans 9:4). Though Israel has in part rejected the Father, the Father has never rejected Israel. As the prodigal son's father ever looked to the horizon for his son's return (Luke 15:20), so God's hands are continually outstretched to this rebellious people (Romans 10:21).

His Word never changes. While it may be possible to imagine a god who is indifferent to the existence of the Jewish people, this is not the God of the Bible, who calls Himself the God of Israel, who loves Israel with an everlasting love (Jeremiah 31:1-3).

Since the God of love never changes, therefore we are to love Israel. Our concern for others, especially Israel, must be based not on our problems with them, but on God's everlasting perspective on them. For just as you once were disobedient to God, but now have been shown mercy because of their disobedience, so these also now have been disobedient, that because of the mercy shown to you they also may now be shown mercy. For God has shut up all in disobedience so that He may show mercy to all" (Romans 11:30-32).

In Romans 11:30 Paul explains verse 11:28a ("from the standpoint of the Good News they are enemies for your sake"); and in 11:31 Paul explains verse 11:28b ("from the standpoint of God's choice they are beloved for the sake of the fathers"). Israel's disobedience, as an enemy, was in order that Gentiles could receive mercy; but that mercy they received was so they could now minister that mercy to Israel, for Israel is beloved.

PURPOSE OF MERCY FOR DISOBEDIENT GENTILES

Gentiles who are now believers were disobedient in the past, just as the nation of Israel is in the present. This is clearly taught in 1 Corinthians 6:9-11 and Romans 1:20. It was not cultural differences but spiritual disobedience, which was the issue. Though the Gentiles did not have the *torah* of Moses, still they knew in their conscience that lying was wrong, yet they lied; and though they knew stealing was wrong, yet they stole (Romans 1:19-20). Immorality, immodesty, and cheating are disobedience to God.

These are not philosophical differences, but disobedience; because it is a matter of truth and what the God of truth desires. When you are under judgment, you need mercy. Those Gentiles who repented had been shown mercy—not a new set of rules, not a new power, but mercy. Through Israel's national rejection of Messiah the Good News was brought to Gentile communities (Acts 8:1, 5; 12:19).

The Fullness of the Gentiles

PURPOSE OF MERCY FROM OBEDIENT GENTILES

Disobedience of Israel is like everyone else's disobedience (same Greek word and tense)—theirs is no worse or more hopeless than anyone else's. As a Gentile believer, you are now to make Jewish people jealous by ministering the same mercy you received from the Lord. When you minister mercy, then you are fulfilling your calling.

Though Gentiles were pagan and disobedient, as Messianic Gentiles they now love the God of Israel. When Jews see Gentiles praising "Christ" it doesn't provoke them to seek mercy. When Jews see Christians carrying crosses, the execution symbol may not communicate Yeshua as much as the way it was misused in the thousands of years in between. Jewish people may not see these as expressions of mercy, any more than you would be drawn to a voodoo event in Haiti. But when Gentiles who were once disobedient pagans now receive mercy from the God of Israel through Messiah, and then glorify Him as such, this is the attraction of mercy.

Those who have received mercy are merciful. While in ministry in New York, I once received a call from Irving, who was a junior high teacher at Brooklyn. He couldn't figure out what had happened to Jose, the custodian at his school. Jose had been a drunk, a gambler, and had a vulgar mouth, but one day Jose came to work a changed man. It was very noticeable; he was now kind and caring.

Jose eventually became a minister in a small Spanish church in East New York. Irving couldn't get over it: Jose had become a follower of Yeshua, and now he was actually being nice to Irving.

Eventually Irving had to have some answers, so he called a Jewish believer in Brooklyn and asked, "Is this what Yeshua did for you as well?" The mercy that Jose had extended to Irving, he found that he wanted too—he wanted what Jose had.

PURPOSE OF MERCY FOR ALL

Paul writes that it was God's purpose to "shut up all in disobedience so that He may show mercy to all" (Romans 11:32). To be "shut up" is a picture of being trapped as in a net.

> But the Scripture has shut up all men under sin, that the promise by faith in Messiah Yeshua might be given to those who believe. (Galatians 3:22)

The Scriptures show our need for mercy. Believers are not people who are better than others. They are merely those people that recognized their spiritually lost situation, and have sought God's mercy in Messiah.

Those who think they are spiritually okay are those who are still lost. Only those who are made desperate enough for mercy are those who find mercy. One purpose of *torah* was to show us our desperate need for Messiah. *Torah* does not make us sinners, any more than a good mirror makes someone ugly; it just reveals us for who we really are—sinners who fall short of the glory of God. "But," you may ask, "will Jewish people accept the Good News message from a Gentile believer?" If you realize that you're drowning, do you care who throws you the life preserver?

Conceit ends when a dependency on mercy begins. We may come to the Lord because of our spiritual thirst: like a dry sponge with nothing to give. But once you've soaked up His grace, you now live to give. Yeshua declares in John 7:37-38,

> All who thirst come to me and drink, and out of your inner being will flow rivers of living water!

Though it may be our thirst that brings us to Yeshua, God fills our lives that we might flow and give to others the very mercy we have received. Thus, Gentile ministry to Israel reveals God's mercy to all. "To Him be the glory forever! Amen." (Romans 11:36).

9

Our Messianic Unity

Therefore, accept one another, just as Messiah also accepted us to the glory of God. (Romans 15:7)

Casey Stengel, legendary manager of the Yankees and later the Mets, said: "It's easy to get good players. Getting them to play together, that's the hard part." It's not easy to accept and serve with others. As in baseball, we may be recruited individually but if we actually play it's as part of a team. You are saved by personal faith, but you live out your salvation as part of a fellowship. As part of just how the Gentiles relate to the Messianic testimony, we will be considering the relationship between Jews and Gentiles in Messiah.

Even as God's triune nature is the basis for all reality, so is life about relationships: friendships, marriages, families, and so on. In context, Paul had been teaching that Jewish and Gentile believers are to accept one another. That is, we are not to judge one another (Romans 14:1-12), and we're not to stumble one another (14:13-23), but rather we're to bear one another's weaknesses (15:1-6).

Our new life by faith in Messiah is the example of acceptance. "Therefore, accept one another just as Messiah has accepted you to the glory of God" (15:7). As He accepted us in heaven, so we are to accept one another on earth. His example of service is our example for living. But how is that possible? Note the word "therefore" (Romans 15:7). As the saying goes, when you see a "therefore" you should see what it's there for! It points us to the context, where we are to accept God's word (15:3-4), His will (15:5-6) and His work for us in Messiah (15:8-12), in order to accept one another—in that order, because His word expresses His will and explains His work for us.

We have unity when we accept that His will for us is in Messiah. In 15:7, the word "accept" is a command. We're commanded to welcome one another. Why? A fragmented *ekklessia* (congregation) isn't any help to a fragmented world. Just as Messiah accepted you, so we also accept one another to God's glory. The history of this relationship has tended towards pressuring Jews to give up their Jewish identity. The pressure (and at times persecution) to remove Jewish expression within the body of Messiah is tragic for a number of biblical reasons, as we have seen. However, this passage of Romans 14-15:7 shows another reason: it reflects a lack of love between Gentiles and Jews and thus a poor testimony. God is glorified in our unity if we accept each other as Messiah did.

What does grace look like when it's at work? Romans 15:8-13 pictures this working grace, God's establishing work for Jew and Gentile alike through Messiah.

TO CONFIRM THE PROMISES

> For I say that Messiah has become a servant to the circumcision on behalf of the truth of God to confirm the promises given to the fathers (Romans 15:8).

"For I say" opens an emphatic clarification regarding how Messiah accepted us. If you do not accept one another "to the glory of God," you are working against Messiah!

Paul first notes that Messiah has become a servant to the circumcision. The concept of circumcision speaks of the Abrahamic covenant, which confirmed the promises of world redemption through Abraham's seed:

And I will make you a great nation, and I will bless you, and make your name great; and so you shall be a blessing; and I will bless those who bless you, and the one who curses you I will curse. And in you all the families of the earth will be blessed. (Genesis 12:2-3; 17:5-9)

Redemptive covenants were made by God only with the Jewish people. Thus, the Lord Yeshua was sent to the lost sheep of the house of Israel alone (Matthew 15:24). Why did Messiah come as Israel's servant? For the truth of God (Messiah) is to confirm the promises given to the fathers, fulfilling and confirming Israel's calling.

The call upon Israel was to bless the world. That call could not be fulfilled apart from Messiah—it all spoke of Him! There was one ministry of Messiah. He came as a Jew to fulfill the prophecies and confirm the promises to Israel. When Paul writes that it was on behalf of the truth of God, he means that Messiah's work was to vindicate the character of God. This ministry to His own people was in the interest of "God's truth" in the sense of God's fidelity to His word, more specifically, His promises made to the patriarchs (Romans 9:4-5; 11:28-29). Messiah's ministry to Israel vindicated God's faithfulness.

In the Greek, the phrase "has become" is in perfect tense. This means it has a past action with a continuing and present result; He became and continues to be a servant of the circumcision; this is Messiah's ongoing service of to Israel. All present service and ministry to the Jewish people demonstrates God's eternal faithfulness to Israel.

Yeshua's ministry was not to conclude the promises, let alone cancel them, but rather to confirm them. Paul's point is that the people of Israel, the Jewish people are not less secure by Messiah's coming and service but even more secure in Him (Jeremiah 31:35-37).

Remember, the promises in Genesis 12:2-3 are that Israel would be a blessing to the world. The promise was that through Messiah, Abraham's seed would bless the world. As Paul wrote in Galatians 3:14, "Messiah redeemed us in order that the blessing given to Abraham might come to the Gentiles through Messiah Yeshua." Thinking globally, God acted locally.

GENTILES GLORIFYING THE GOD OF ISRAEL

And for the Gentiles to glorify God for His mercy as it is written, "therefore I will give praise to you among the Gentiles, and I will sing to your name." Again he says, "Rejoice, O Gentiles, with His people." And again, "praise the Lord all you Gentiles, and let all the peoples praise Him." Again Isaiah says, "There shall come the root of Jesse, and He who arises to rule over the Gentiles, in him shall the Gentiles hope." (Romans 15:9-12)

The quotations here are from various portions of *Tanakh* (through the Greek Septuagint).

- Verse 9 is taken from 2 Samuel 22:50 in the former prophets, as well as Psalm 18:49 from the writings.
- The verse quoted in 15:10 is from Deuteronomy 32:43 in the Pentateuch.
- In verse 11, the quotation is from Psalm 117:1.
- Finally, verse 12 quotes Isaiah, one of the latter prophets (Isaiah 11:1, 10).

There is a point in these selections. They show how the Hebrew Bible as a whole—*Torah*, *Nevi'im* (prophets), and *Ketuvim* (writings)—testifies that the Gentiles were to be ministering alongside the Jewish people. God wants Israel to preach His mercy to the Gentiles so that we all praise His name together, eventually under His literal reign (Genesis 49:10; Isaiah 11:10; Romans 15:12).

Paul's calling to minister to the Gentiles represented Israel's calling from the Abrahamic covenant to bless the nations. His only ministry to Gentiles was through God's promises to Israel. In confirming the promises to Israel, Messiah made salvation available for Gentiles to glorify God for His mercy. It is the confirmed promises that continue to validate ministry to the Gentiles. When God's calling to Israel ceases, then His mercy to the Gentiles ceases. His ministry to Israel was and is God's way of reaching the world, because if the promises to Israel were canceled, ministry to the world would be as well.

Our unique unity thus makes demands on both Jews and Gentiles: Jewish believers accept the confirmed promises to reach out to the Gentiles, and as Gentile believers accept the confirmed promises to Israel, they then minister mercy back to them (Romans 11:11, 31). This was a further "to the Jew first" reminder to the Gentile believers that God had given priority to Israel, so that the Gentiles might have mercy and hope in Yeshua.

Our work is to be modeled on God's work; all authentic spiritual work is incarnational. Yeshua sends us into the world, as the Father sent Him into the world (John 20:21). We trust Him for unity, and experience that unity in Messiah.

Gentile believers, minister to our people as Messiah did, confirming and not canceling the promises to the fathers. How? By becoming a servant to the circumcised (Romans 15:8). All promises were for the unifying of peoples in Messiah, a unity not experienced since Adam, since Babel, and since the Law revealed our failures. As Gentile believers heed the call and follow Messiah, they are confirmed in ministry to Israel.

Yet again, God called and uses Israel to minister His mercy in Messiah to Gentiles. God also uses saved Gentiles to serve and make Israel jealous, through the mercy they had received through Israel. To God be the glory!

May His name endure forever;
May His name increase as long as the sun shines;
And let men bless themselves by him,
Let all Nations call Him blessed.

Psalm 72:17

10

Jewish Good News for Gentiles

We are complete in Messiah. Knowing Him brings about the transformation and satisfaction of our souls, which is true spirituality. Still, there are those stories of Gentiles who have converted to traditional Judaism, occasionally even using "Messianic Judaism" as a stepping stone. Somehow, Yeshua was not enough for them. Decisions like this are made from poor discipleship, reflecting a lack of sound teaching in the Word of God. The completed work necessary for salvation and perfect fellowship with God has been accomplished eternally in Messiah, that we might be "a praise to the glory of His grace" (Ephesians 1:14). In Messiah, people who were spiritually dead toward God, at the moment of faith are by His grace made spiritually alive; not *by* good works, but *for* good works (Ephesians 2:1-10).

Simultaneous to that reality of salvation, Gentile believers are made one with Jewish believers in Messiah (Ephesians 2:11-22). This unity is a spiritual revelation that was not previously known (Ephesians 3:1-13). Paul hopes that all believers might be strengthened in that love "that they might be filled with the fullness of God" (Ephesians 3:14-21). This revelation of Jewish and Gentile unity is important enough to explore further; we might dare say that it *is* the testimony of Yeshua in our lives.

GENTILES WERE "WITHOUT"

Paul goes on to explain how the Gentile's spiritual past was grievous without Messiah:

> Therefore remember that formerly you, the Gentiles in the flesh, who are called "Uncircumcision" by the so-called "Circumcision," which is performed in the flesh by human hands—remember that you were at that time separate from Messiah, excluded from the commonwealth of Israel, and strangers to the covenants of promise, having no hope and without God in the world. (Ephesians 2:11-12)

The (non-Messianic) Jewish community despised Gentiles as uncircumcised pagans. It was unacceptable for any observant Jewish person to associate with Gentiles. This is why Peter needed a vision from God to minister to Cornelius, a Gentile "God-fearer"; mixing was simply not proper or good. Peter would later have to explain why he would go to a Gentile home, and either have to explain himself or face censure from the other believers (Acts 10-11).

Thus, the Gentile's spiritual situation before coming to faith in Yeshua is characterized as "without." The Gentile is without Messiah, separated from the true vine of Israel (John 15:5). The Gentile is without citizenship, excluded from commonwealth of Israel, with no benefits in the community of God. The Gentile is without promises, since as we have seen, all covenants of promise were made with Israel. The Gentile is without hope. To those without hope, reality is despair. It is like trying to survive without breath. Finally, the Gentile is without God Himself. They are, as the saying goes, "up the creek without a paddle."

So lost and deceived was the Gentile world that they were generally unaware of this state, with no idea of any hope or promise. Though the Jews did have all these things, apart from the promise we were lost as well; in reality, all fall short (Romans 3:23).

WELCOME TO THE COMMONWEALTH

By faith in Messiah, the Gentile's situation changes. While most of the ways it changes have often been well understood in traditional Christian commentaries, one area where many seem to be unclear is "the commonwealth of Israel" which includes Gentiles. Some have tended to spiritualize the matter, making the commonwealth of Israel equal to "the church" in keeping with Covenant theology, whereas others have made it merely a political matter for the millennial kingdom in keeping with Dispensationalism. Some have also taken this phrase to imply that Gentiles become Israelites. To understand its meaning, we are indebted to the insights provided by Messianic writers (e.g., Dan Juster's *Jewish Roots*, David Stern's commentary, Dan Gruber, *The Church and the Jews*).

"Commonwealth" (*politeias*) is used a few times in the New Covenant writings (Acts 22:28; Philippians 3:20). The idea of "commonwealth" should not be taken to refer to the nation of Israel. While the distinction may seem subtle, the Greek word for the commonwealth is never used for "nation" (*goy* in Hebrew, *ethnos* in Greek). However, it is used to mean "citizenship." Thus, in Acts 22:28 Paul and a Roman soldier had the same rights because of shared Roman citizenship (*politeias*), even though they were not of a shared nationality (*ethnos*). The idea of commonwealth is that of citizenship in a community which transcends national borders.

The core issue wasn't exclusion from the nation of Israel, but from the life of the people of Israel, "the well-being of the community." As believers in Messiah Yeshua, Jewish and Gentile people do not share the same nationality, but they share the same rights, values, and relationship with the living God. Moreover, this is a reality that is happening *now*, not only when the Kingdom on earth is established at Messiah's return. Paul is indeed saying that in times past Gentiles were not fellow citizens, but that now, along with Jewish believers, they are!

As a Jewish nation, citizenship also included the idea of community, way of life, and national life. In the US, citizenship is a legal issue, while the cultural issues are hotly debated. However, as a spiritual theocracy, Biblical Israel's commonwealth included cultural, social, legal, religious and spiritual matters. Whereas for us, the issue of citizenship carries with it the idea of "rights and privileges," there is even more expressed here: sharing in fellowship, a common set of values and way of life (Ephesians 2:19).

This is the Gentile's true spiritual unity within the body of Messiah and identification with Israel: not being Jewish, yet a part of (invested in and interested in the welfare of) Jewish life. They are intertwined with Jews as part of the Biblical community of God.

Consider an analogy to the *modern* Jewish state of Israel. The Law of Return is for those with Hebrew ancestry; those with at least one Jewish grandparent have the right to citizenship. However, in addition to this, the Gentile spouse of an Israeli citizen may make *aliyah* (immigrate) and receive citizenship as well. While this does not change her ethnicity, he or she might just enjoy *Yom Ha'atzma'ut* (Independence Day) and other national holidays, appreciating the state as much as, and possibly more than, those who were born in the land.

In a similar way, though Israel's deliverance from bondage in Egypt is a freedom celebrated by the Jewish people, Gentile believers can enjoy Passover every bit as much as any Jewish believer. They may find it more meaningful than Jewish people who do not know Passover's fulfillment in Yeshua. How remarkably strange that Gentiles would be cut off, by anti-Jewish tradition, from remembering Messiah through Passover! How wonderful to see this pattern of estrangement often reversed in our generation!

This inclusion in the commonwealth of Israel gives Gentile believers their relation to the Jewish people in service and witness (Romans 11:11, 31). The truth that Yeshua is the Messiah of Israel would be difficult, if not impossible, to communicate without showing the Jewish Biblical relevance that Yeshua brings to Jew and Gentile alike. Gentile inclusion into the Messianic way demonstrates God's grace.

> But now in Messiah Yeshua you who formerly were far off have been brought near by the blood of Messiah. (Ephesians 2:13)

Being "without" these various blessings in 2:12 is considered simply as Gentiles being "far off." The terms "far" and "near," used here and in verse 17, allude to the offerings in the Temple. The word for "offering" in Hebrew is *korban*, from the word *karav*, which means "to approach or come near" to someone. In offering the proper sacrifice, the worshipper came near or approached God through the offering. Though sin separated the worshipper from God, the offering appeased God's wrath toward sin so that one could draw near to Him. The Gentiles did not have the Temple and offerings to approach, so they were considered far off. Through the sacrifices, Jewish people had "front row seats" for an audience with the King. The Gentiles were not even in the building!

NO BORDER LINES

It must be stressed, therefore, that it was not ethnicity or nationality that made Gentiles far off, but rather their sin. Sin makes everyone far off. Even of Jewish people it was written, "your sins have made a separation between you and your God" (Isaiah 59:1-2). Through the atonement foreshadowed by the sacrificial system, Messiah paid the price to have you close to Him, and not far off.

> For He Himself is our peace, who made both groups into one and broke down the barrier of the dividing wall, by abolishing in His flesh the enmity, which is the Law of commandments contained in ordinances. (Ephesians 2:14-15a)

137

Being brought near by Messiah makes Gentile believers as near as Jewish believers are to God, but also makes Gentiles one with Jewish believers! How does God make us one? "For He Himself is our peace." Messiah is *Sar Shalom*, the "Prince of Peace" (Isaiah 9:6); He is our peace with God (Romans 5:1), our peace of mind (Philippians 4:6-7), and our peace with one another (Ephesians 2:14, above).

How is Messiah "our peace" in this verse? He is our *peace offering*. In the *Tanakh*, an offering was at times referred to by its distinctive. For example, the sin offering may just be called "sin" (Leviticus 4:20; 2 Corinthians 5:21). Yeshua fulfills all of the offerings, in that they all point to Him. Here in Ephesians, Paul refers to the peace offering as our "peace."

The *shalam* or peace offering indicated that there was complete peace with God—a completeness you would share with the other worshippers. The offering was actually eaten by those offering the sacrifice, and this brought them together in fellowship, making them one. That's why the Scripture says that "Gentiles are fellow heirs, and fellow members of the body, and fellow partakers of His promise in Messiah Yeshua through the Good News" (Ephesians 3:6; Hebrews 3:14). By faith we trust in and partake of His sacrifice for our sins.

It is a little like the old western movies, where they smoked the peace pipe together: no one smoked it alone. Please notice present tense in the phrase: "He *is* our peace." He is presently able to bring peace to you now. There's a Jewish saying: "Whosoever offers a peace offering sacrifice brings peace to the world." Such was God's peace offering in the death of Messiah. Thus Messiah is our peace offering, where the participants enjoyed fellowship eating the offering together (Leviticus 7:15). He can bring peace to you and to the whole world.

Paul writes of several partitions that Yeshua removes to make us one in Himself: "the dividing wall," "the enmity," and the "commandments contained in ordinances" (Ephesians

2:14b-15a). Outside the Jerusalem Temple courts was a partition wall known as the *soreg*. This was the barrier beyond which Gentiles were not permitted to approach the Temple area. At the *soreg* was posted an inscription:

> No foreigner may enter within the barricade which surrounds the sanctuary and enclosure. Anyone who is caught doing so will have himself to blame for his ensuing death.

In the Temple area, there were actually several partitions: the outer wall, separating the Gentile proselytes from access to the court of the Jews; the inner wall, severing the Jewish people from entrance to the holy part of the temple where the priests officiated; and even an inner veil that separated the priests from the Lord. In Messiah, these have all been removed, and there is access for all into the presence of God! This means we are one, all together before Him. If, in Messiah, there is no dividing veil between God and man, then, if we are found in Messiah, there is no dividing wall between any of us as well. The grace that makes us one with the Lord makes us one with each other!

A NEW MAN, RECONCILED AND RESTORED

"Enmity" can mean hostility, hatred, animosities, discord, or feuds. Even as the *soreg* represented the Mosaic separation between Jews and Gentiles, we saw before in chapter 5 that the enmity itself was a righteous result of the *torah*. According to Leviticus 18:24 the idolatrous, pagan nations were considered defiled; therefore, any interaction with them was ceremonially defiling for Israel. This is why we read in Joshua 23:6-7, "do all that is written in the book of the law of Moses … so that you will not associate with these nations." Association with Gentiles would be like stepping in mud. The rabbis decreed that clods of dirt from Gentile lands were to be burnt on the possibility that they might ceremonially defile one's offerings (Shabbat 15b). Using a play on words, the Talmud connects the hatred for the nations to the meaning of Sinai itself:

> For R. Hisda and Rabba the son of R. Huna both said, "What is [the meaning of] Mount *Sinai*? The mountain whereon there descended hostility [*sin'ah*, lit. "hatred"] toward idolaters" (Shabbat 89a).

This mandated division between the people of God and the nations led to enmity. Segregation emphasizes differences, and in a fallen world produces a hatred and derision of those who are different.

By Messiah's death, He put an end to the hostility that separated Jews and Gentiles (Ephesians 2:14). In reconciling us to God, all reconciliation has been provided. To what end did Messiah remove the enmity?

> So that in Himself He might make the two into one new man, thus establishing peace, even as Yeshua established peace, might reconcile them both in one body to God through the cross, by it having put to death the enmity. (Ephesians 2:15b-16)

This new man is a relationship that is only possible through the New Covenant, a spiritual unity which is beyond nationality. Even as God would unite the ever-warring nations of Israel and Judah through the New Covenant (Jeremiah 31:31-34), so this same God unites Jews and Gentiles.

There's a new place of unity: "in Himself." Messiah is our refuge from the wrath of God, but also the place of eternal unity with God, and with all other believers. The ground is level at the cross.

Paul says that this work of Yeshua results in "establishing peace," or *shalom*. This *shalom* of God is more than just a cessation to hostilities, but the true fullness of our purpose, what was desired for us when He created us in His image. By relating to HaShem we fulfill our calling to represent His eternal values, love and life. Its not being transported out of the world, but living Him out where we are.

The death of Messiah restores us to God because His death removes the penalty, grief, and separation of sin. Those who were far off because of sin, which is everyone, may now be brought near to God. The enmity did not begin with the Mosaic Law, but in the Garden of Eden; the *torah* merely brought the enmity to the surface. From the very first sin, we have had enmity towards our Maker. So also, God's righteous wrath against sinners reveals His enmity against sin. Thus Paul states in Romans 1:18, "For the wrath of God is revealed from heaven against all ungodliness and unrighteousness of men." From the Garden of Eden forward, restoration was needed. In restoring us to unity with our Maker, Messiah's redemption would restore believing humanity to one another as well.

The work of the cross is the destruction of everything that has caused disunity. All has been accomplished in Messiah, and in Him "you (*pl.*) have been made complete" (Colossians 2:10). As Paul has written, "Therefore, having been justified by faith, we have peace with God through Messiah Yeshua our Lord" (Romans 5:1). You are at peace with God in Messiah, and you are complete in Him, so to attempt to improve on that is to demean His perfect salvation for you (Galatians 5:6).

We are reconciled to God, and one with each other by trusting in Messiah's atoning work. Hence, there is one body (Ephesians 4:4); when you came to faith in Yeshua you were immediately made one with every other believer on planet Earth, and in Heaven. By His sacrifice, Yeshua has removed the partitions, and by His grace, He makes us one.

At a duck farm, various breeds of ducks were separated by fences. One day a heavy rain came and the ponds overflowed the fences that had previously kept the ducks separate. By this 'overflow' they now became one flock. Similarly, in Yeshua's flood of grace, the partitions are removed and all believers are one in Him. Hence, we are not to rebuild barriers. Division comes from not relying upon God's sufficient grace.

ACCEPTED FOR ACCESS, AIMING FOR A NEW ABODE

As a result of this unity, the Gentile believer in Yeshua has new privileges which cannot possibly be overstated.

> And He came and preached peace to you who were far away, and peace to those who were near; for through Him we both have our access in one Spirit to the Father. (Ephesians 2:17-18)

Paul notes that this access was promised in Isaiah 57:19, "He (Messiah) came and preached peace," simply stating that the way to God is proclaimed in Yeshua. Those who are far are never too far for God to save; those who are near are never near enough not to need God's grace and mercy. His message of forgiveness for sins and reconciliation with God is for both Jews and Gentiles, for all fall short of His glory (Romans 3:23).

Throughout Messiah's ministry, He called people to Himself: those who were thirsty, weary and heavy laden, with the promise of rest and peace (Matthew 11:28; John 7:37). Even after Messiah's death and resurrection, He preached this message through the apostles, as He does today by His Spirit through all who follow Him (Matthew 28:20; Luke 24:46-48; Acts 1:8). Please note that the three Persons of the Triune God are involved: "for through Him"—Messiah is the Door and the Way—"we both have our access in one Spirit to the Father."

> So then you are no longer strangers and aliens, but you are fellow citizens with the saints, and are of God's household. (Ephesians 2:19)

My how things have changed! Paul uses two terms that are synonyms, "strangers and aliens." They both refer to the idea of being alienated, but there is a difference. "Strangers" (*xenoi*) applies to short-term transients; they are moving through, never develop long-term relationships, and therefore are considered strange and different. The word for "aliens" (*paroikos*) has long term intent. They were the *resident* aliens who had settled in the country, but had no rights as citizens. Yet now Gentiles are "fellow citizens with the saints and members of the household of God" (Ephesians 2:19). His point is that their 'horizontal' citizenship alongside Jewish believers is 'vertically' identified with the household of God. This provides an answer for the beginning of the verse, "So then you are no longer strangers and aliens." Gentile believers are not strangers, but citizens, and not aliens, but family members.

The irony is that in being made near to God we are now counted as being far from the world, which is in rebellion. On this point, Peter writes,

> Beloved, I urge you as aliens and strangers to abstain from fleshly lusts which wage war against the soul. (1 Peter 2:11)

Here the point is that we are "aliens and strangers" to the world. Thus we are told by Jacob that "friendship with the world is enmity with God" (Jacob 4:4). And John writes: "Love not the world, nor the things of the world, for who desires the love of the world, the love of the Father dwells not in him" (1 John 2:15). But in Messiah there is infinitely more gained than lost.

> ...having been built on the foundation of the apostles and prophets, Messiah Yeshua Himself being the corner stone, in whom the whole building, being fitted together, is growing into a holy temple in the Lord, in whom you also are being built together into a dwelling of God in the Spirit. (Ephesians 2:20-22)

There is ultimately only one dwelling for God: the human dwelling he has made for Himself, a temple not made with hands. Please notice the past tense of having been built, and that upon this proper foundation we are to build (v. 20). We are God's household, or house, being built upon one foundation that has already been laid. This foundation is the authoritative teaching ministry of the apostles, with the authoritative affirming work of the prophets. The apostles were the messengers sent to proclaim Yeshua (Luke 24:46-49); the prophets preached that apostolic message with conviction to the hearts of the people (1 Corinthians 14:24-25).

Yeshua, and the teaching about Him, is the cornerstone of the faith. The word "cornerstone" (in Hebrew *even pina* or *rosh pina*) is found in the key Messianic texts of Psalm 118:22 and Isaiah 28:16, as well as in the New Covenant in Luke 20:17 and 1 Peter 2:6. It refers to the foundation stone by which both Jewish and Gentile "sides" are united in the same building.

You establish a foundation only once (Ephesians 2:20). If it is properly established the first time, no other foundation is needed: no other "apostles" need apply. Believers have equal access to God by the same Spirit, not because of any activity or permission of any present, earthly leaders, but because of the past authoritative foundation already laid in Yeshua. If we are going to be built up at all, we must let our present activities of love and acceptance harmonize with that teaching.

In the real estate world, the three most important words are: *location, location, location*! Yeshua is always the right location for growth. The right fitting upon this foundation is essential —"in whom" we are being fitted together (Ephesians 2:21). The phrase "in whom" refers to the function of the cornerstone (Ephesians 2:20). Our alignment in Him determines our being fitted together. Our lives together are one in Messiah.

If we are rightly relating to the Head, then as we are accepted before God, so we will accept one another and be rightly aligned with each other. This is the means of growth into holiness. Otherwise, there's no holiness, and as God's dwelling there's no growth either.

We are the Temple that God is building. In the early centuries, Messianic believers had no physical buildings of their own, but this did not hurt the growth of the Body. The true temple is the whole congregation of believers. The term "dwelling" is used frequently to denote God's "dwelling place" either on earth or in heaven (1 Kings 8:39; Psalm 76:2). Now

God makes His abode in the body of believers, prefiguring a glorious future which John described:

> And I saw the holy city, new Jerusalem, coming down out of heaven from God, made ready as a bride adorned for her husband. And I heard a loud voice from the throne, saying, "Behold, the tabernacle of God is among men, and He will dwell among them, and they shall be His people, and God Himself will be among them. (Revelation 21:2-3)

The aim of the process is that the Body should become God's holy residence. If God, through Messiah's atonement, can dwell with sinful man, then through that same atonement, we ought to be able to dwell with one another. Are we growing as a holy temple in all reverence and love? It is our goal as the Body of Messiah, Jews and Gentiles together in Yeshua. This is a glorious matter to God.

In the book *Peace Child,* Don Richardson records the moving account of how the Sawi people of Irian Jaya came to understand salvation through Yeshua. For many months he and his family sought for some way to communicate the Good News to this tribe. Then they discovered the key for which they had been praying. All demonstrations of kindness expressed by the Sawi were regarded with suspicion except for one act. If a father gave his own son to his enemy, his sacrificial deed showed that he could be trusted. Furthermore, everyone who touched that child was brought into a friendly relationship with the father. The family then taught the Sawi that, in a similar way, the beloved Son could bring them not only peace with their enemies, but peace with the Father as well. Your acceptance in Messiah is evidenced in your acceptance of one another.

Part Three

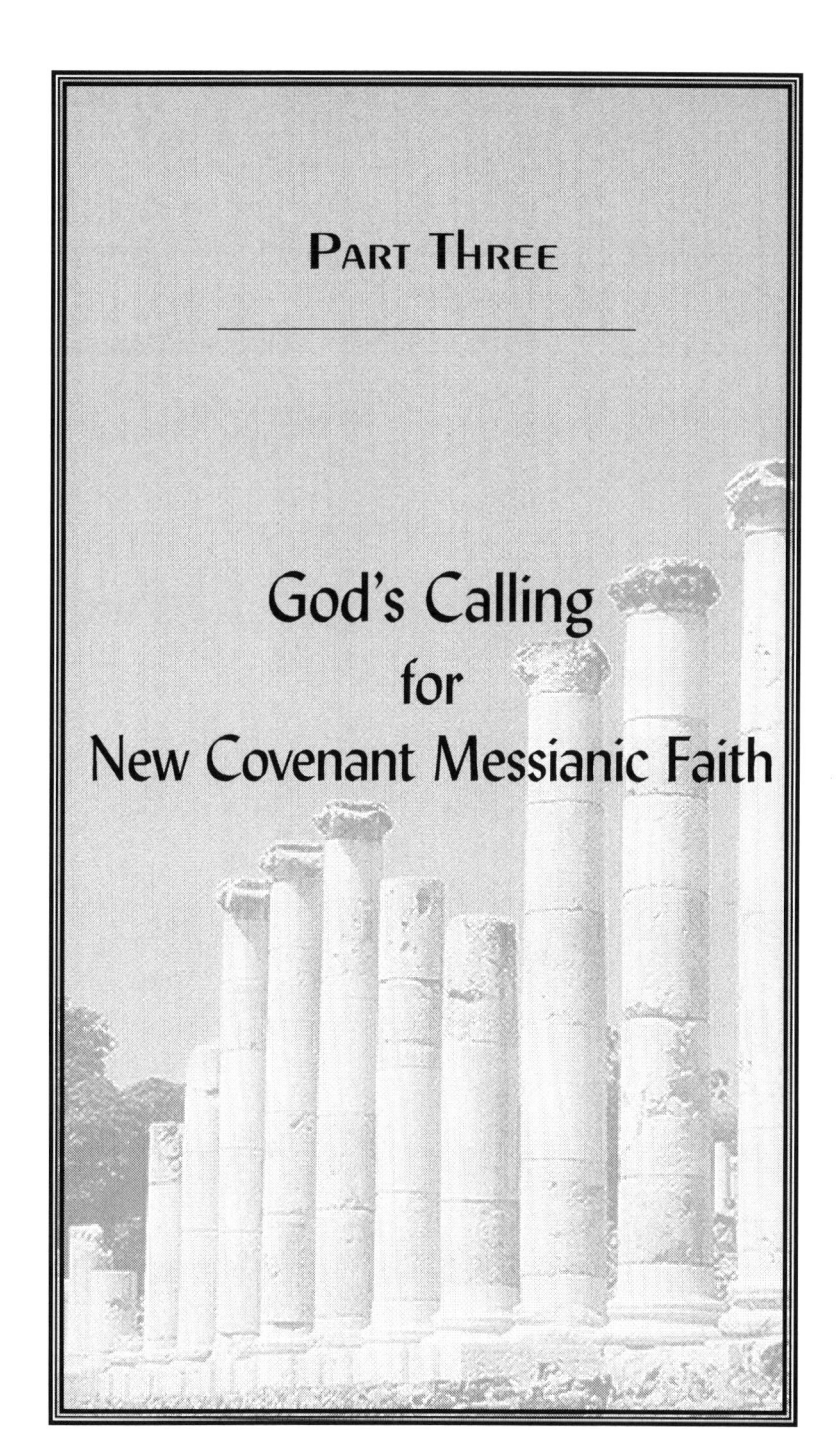

God's Calling for New Covenant Messianic Faith

Behold, as for the proud one, his soul is not right within him; but the righteous will live by his faith.

Habakkuk 2:4

11

NEW COVENANT ORIENTATION

We have considered God's calling upon the Jewish people in Messiah: how the remnant of Israel visibly expresses God's faithfulness, and how faith in Yeshua alone is the Jewish means of salvation. Then we considered God's calling upon Gentile believers. They are to make Israel jealous; though they do not replace Israel, they identify with Israel in love and service, sharing a unique spiritual unity with Jewish believers as part of the family of God. The idea is that this was really a Jewish thing from the beginning, and still is. Yet there are major issues for our practice which need to be discerned.

In the Messianic world, there is much discussion about the believer's relationship to *torah*. However, though we sometimes speak about it loosely ("Does your congregation keep *torah*?"), the notion really needs to be understood in its covenant context. By understanding covenants, we can understand *torah*.

A covenant (or *brit* in Hebrew) is a binding agreement among two or more parties. To accomplish His plan of redemption, God promised to establish a New Covenant with His people Israel. The New Covenant demonstrates itself to be the fulfillment of what the *Tanakh* had promised, and as such establishes our faith in Messiah.

A NEW COVENANT PROMISED

We see hints, even foreshadows, of the New Covenant in the second covenant given through Moses to Israel. This covenant was given "in the land of Moab, besides the covenant that he made with them in Horeb [Mt. Sinai]" (Deuteronomy 29-30). There we read the promise of a future "circumcision of the heart," given so that we could truly "love God" and fulfill our calling as His people (Deuteronomy 30:6).

The prophets who succeeded Moses did not see themselves as contradicting or replacing him, of course. Rather they understood their ministries as building upon what Moses had written, applying the *torah* of Mt. Sinai to their time. So, reflecting back on Deuteronomy, Ezekiel saw a "new heart and new spirit," given that we might be able to live out God's truth (Ezekiel 36:26-27). The prophet Jeremiah further developed this into the most direct statement on the New Covenant (Jeremiah 31:31-34). God's culminating work for humanity would provide a better relationship through a better agreement.

Some have implied since we now have a New Covenant, the Mosaic covenant (and its *torah*) is irrelevant. Others have downplayed the notion of a *New* Covenant at all, viewing it rather as a "renewed" covenant, which simply enables us to better follow Moses. In the following chapters we will look closely at Jeremiah 31:31-34, in the process setting out some guidelines for a New Covenant orientation and its provisions. This chapter will consider the newness and difference of this covenant.

A NEW COVENANT FOR AN ANCIENT PEOPLE

Jeremiah has a startling announcement, "Behold! I will make a new covenant with the house of Israel and the house of Judah" (Jeremiah 31:31). "New covenant" in Hebrew is *brit chadasha*. Some have raised the question, "Is it a new or renewed covenant?" and others have argued for translating it as "renewed covenant." It should be noted that there really is not a word for the adjective "renewed" in Greek or Hebrew. While the Hebrew verb *chadesh* can mean either "to make new" or "to renew," the adjective means "new," with only one possible exception (Job 29:20). Thus, we would need very good overriding evidence to consider it as something besides "new." In the absence of that, we should go with the clear sense of Hebrew and in the Greek Septuagint (*chadash*, *kainos*), where "new" simply means new.

The New Covenant Scriptures pick up this Greek term for "new," for example, "this cup… is the new covenant in My blood" (Luke 22:20; 1 Corinthians 11:25; 2 Corinthians 3:6; Hebrews 8:8, 13; 9:15). The Greek verb "renewed" was also normally used (Romans 12:2; 2 Corinthians 4:16; Ephesians 4:23, and so on), but never to refer to the New Covenant.

Perhaps more striking is that all modern Jewish translations translate *brit chadasha* in Jeremiah 31:31 as "new covenant." In light of its usage today by followers of Yeshua, translating it "renewed covenant" would have apologetic value for traditional Judaism, but it is not translated as such because that would not be accurate to the text in context. Therefore, *brit chadasha* is properly translated "new covenant."

Some have argued that the New Covenant must be in some sense a renewal, since the Mosaic covenant is *brit olam*, an Everlasting Covenant (Exodus 31:16). Though *olam* can be understood as "indefinite," the Mosaic covenant is everlasting, but we must not miss the broader point: All covenants from God are everlasting, or eternal. We see this in the following:

- ✡ Noahic covenant (Genesis 9:16; Isaiah 24:5);
- ✡ Abrahamic covenant (Genesis 17:7; 1 Chronicles 16:17; Psalm 105:10);
- ✡ Mosaic covenant (also Sinai, Horeb, and First, since it was the first made with Israel; Exodus 31:16; Leviticus 24:8);
- ✡ Davidic covenant (2 Samuel 23:5);
- ✡ New Covenant (Isaiah 55:3; 61:8; Jeremiah 32:40; 50:5; Ezekiel 16:60; 37:26; Hebrews 9:15; 13:20; Revelation 14:6).

Covenants are *olam*, or everlasting, because of the eternal and everlasting values they reveal; the Eternal One can only do that which reflects and reveals eternal truth. Hence all Scripture is not only inspired, but is always profitable, applicable, and generally helpful in living our lives as God meant them to be lived—for His glory. The values contained in all Scripture are eternal values, for the Scriptures themselves are eternally inspired (2 Timothy 3:15-17). However, while God is eternal, we are not; He does not change, but we do. Thus, our relationship to these covenants may change as well.

In traditional Judaism, the application of *torah* is authoritatively found in the Talmud, Midrash, and other rabbinical literature. The "oral law" is meant to fulfill a need in the community, providing authoritative application of the Written Law. Thus, tradition recognizes the necessity for authoritative application of the Scriptures, which is also called *halacha* (or "walk").

As followers of Messiah, our *halacha* is found in the teaching of Messiah and His *shlichim* (Apostles). New Covenant *halacha* helps us understand how Yeshua "came not to destroy but to fulfill the Law and Prophets" (Matthew 5:17-18). In Messiah the righteous goal of the Mosaic *torah* is fulfilled (Romans 10:4).

A DIFFERENT COVENANT FOR A RELIGIOUS PEOPLE

However, in this case, we may wonder: what is so "new" about the New Covenant? We read that the New Covenant is:

> ... not like the covenant which I made with their fathers in the day I took them by the hand to bring them out of the land of Egypt, My covenant which they broke, although I was a husband to them, declares the LORD. (Jeremiah 31:32)

The text states that the New Covenant is "not like the covenant" (*lo kabrit*) made at Mt Sinai when Israel came out of Egypt. "New" does not in this case merely mean novel or recent, nor does it mean the same covenant but in a different location (that is, on the heart rather than on tablets). Rather, this covenant is different.

The Mosaic covenant was breakable, because it is a *conditional* covenant. This matter "bookends" the part of the first five books of Moses that deals with Sinai covenant and law, near their beginning in Exodus 19 and their conclusion in Deuteronomy 28. At the beginning of this part we read:

> "Now then, if you will indeed obey My voice and keep My covenant, then you shall be My own possession among all the peoples, for all the earth is Mine; and you shall be to Me a kingdom of priests and a holy nation." These are the words that you shall speak to the sons of Israel. (Exodus 19:5-6)

This "if-then" statement presents a conditional agreement. *If* the conditions are met, *then* the benefits are gained: but not apart from the conditions being met. Obeying God's voice is necessary before we can be His own possession; "a kingdom of priests, and a holy nation." At the conclusion we read:

> Now it shall be, if you diligently obey the Lord your God, being careful to do all His commandments which I command you today, then the Lord your God will set you high above all the nations of the earth. All these blessings will come upon you and overtake you if you obey the Lord your God. (Deuteronomy 28:1-2)

The twelve following verses detail the blessings of obedience. However, the blessings are gained upon hearing God's voice and obeying His commands. Not just hearing His voice, but diligently listening (*shimoah tishmah*) to His voice. And not just 'obeying' His commands, but diligently doing (*lishmor la'asot*) His commands. And not just diligently obeying some of His commands, but diligently obeying all of His commands. Only then the benefits kick in.

"And what if I don't?" We then see the results of disobedience under the Mosaic Covenant:

> But it shall come about, if you do not obey the Lord your God, to observe to do all His commandments and His statutes with which I charge you today, that all these curses will come upon you and overtake you. (Deuteronomy 28:15)

The fifty-three following verses contain the curses which will come about if strict obedience to His commandments is not followed (Deuteronomy 28:16-68). If you did not obey, according to this covenant, then these curses will come upon you. It may seem harsh for curses to come upon someone for breaking just one command. But realize that the curses come upon you not because you broke one command but because in breaking one command the whole covenant was broken: it is an "all or nothing at all" covenant. Would God not bless His people, as flawed as we are? Yes, He would, but only on the basis of His mercy and grace, *not* on the basis of our inadequate obedience. Though the purposes of the Mosaic covenant are profound indeed, the major purpose was to show us His holiness, and therefore our need for repentance and His forgiveness. It shows that the promises given to Abraham were on the basis of grace, which would ultimately lead us to the greater seed of Abraham, who is also the prophet like unto Moses: Messiah Yeshua.

ABRAHAMIC AND MOSAIC COVENANTS COMPARED

In this regard I am continually struck by the unconditional blessings for Abraham. It seems Moses himself was impressed! When the law at Mt. Sinai was first given to Moses, something occurred there which we call "the Golden Calf incident." The Law revealed the people as idolaters and worthy of the severest judgment (Exodus 32:9-10). So when God determined to wipe us out as a people, Moses interceded for us — not by reminding HaShem of the covenant he had just received from Him on the Mount; but on the basis of the Abrahamic covenant!

Remember Abraham, Isaac, and Israel, Your servants to whom You swore by Yourself, and said to them, "I will multiply your descendants as the stars of the heavens, and all this land of which I have spoken I will give to your descendants, and they shall inherit it forever." (Exodus 32:13)

The Scripture then notes in 32:14, "So the LORD changed His mind about the harm which He said He would do to His people."

Our people, even under Moses, were not secured by the Mosaic Covenant. With the giving of the *torah* of Moses, the Golden Calf was now revealed to be idolatry and condemnatory sin. The Mosaic covenant revealed us to be sinners. It revealed our desperate need for mercy and grace from God, and compelled us to approach Him through the Abrahamic Covenant for our security as a people. This unconditional nature is the basis for the hope of the "second covenant" made at Moab (Deuteronomy 29:1), as well as the foundation of the New Covenant that has been established in Messiah (Galatians 3:14). For as Abraham was unconditionally promised the land, so Mosaic law declared living in the land was a matter of obedience (Genesis 12:1, 7; 13:14-17; Deuteronomy 28:63-65).

The second covenant from Deuteronomy 29-30 reiterates the lack in the Mosaic covenant. Though the Law had been given, "yet to this day the LORD has not given you a heart to know, nor eyes to see, nor ears to hear" (Deuteronomy 29:4). Therefore our disobedience would remove us from the land.

> All the nations will say, 'why has the Lord done thus to this land? Why this great outburst of anger?' Then men will say, 'because they forsook the covenant of the Lord, the God of their fathers, which He made with them when He brought them out of the land of Egypt. They went and served other gods and worshiped them, gods whom they have not known and whom He had not allotted to them. Therefore, the anger of the Lord burned against that land, to bring upon it every curse which is written in this book. (Deuteronomy 29:24-27)

The promise that God will bring us back to the Land will find its fulfillment in the future (Deuteronomy 30:3-5). Moses assures our people that following our return to the Lord with repentance of heart, we will then obey Him fully. This faith-obedience spoken of in Deuteronomy 30 is ultimately seen in our national obedience to Messiah and His Good News (Hosea 3:5; Zechariah 12:10; John 3:36; Romans 10:6-9; 16:25-26). This return to the Lord is identified with our return to the Land, so as to then fully possess it. How would it be possible to obey the Lord in the future, if it were not possible to obey Him now? Though at that time God had not given them "a heart to know" (Deuteronomy 29:4), upon repentance and faith in Messiah, God "will circumcise" our hearts so that as a nation we might truly live (Deuteronomy 30:6).

In the Abrahamic covenant there was the promise of the seed to be like the dust of the earth, stars of the heavens, and sand on the seashore (Genesis 12:2; 13:16; 17:4, 22:17-18, etc). In the Mosaic Covenant, there was the promise that without full obedience that seed would become "few in number" (Deuteronomy 28:62). This will be reversed again, so God will "prosper abundantly … the offspring of your body" (Deuteronomy 30:9).

In the Abrahamic covenant there was the promise of the blessing, not only for the seed of Abraham, but through that seed to "all the nations of the earth" (Genesis 12:3, 22:18). The law of Moses assures our people that without full obedience to "all His commandments" there would not be blessings, but curses (Deuteronomy 28:15). Rather than be a blessing to the nations we would be a sign to the nations of judgment for disobedience (Deuteronomy 29:24-28). For the nations will not be blessed until the seed of Abraham honors the Lord, as Jeremiah agreed,

> And you will swear, "As the LORD lives," in truth, in justice and in righteousness; then the nations will be blessed in Him, and in Him they will glory. (Jeremiah 4:2)

This reversal back to blessing, after heart circumcision, is promised in the second covenant "that you may live and multiply, and that the Lord your God may bless you in the land where you are entering to possess it" (Deuteronomy 30:16).

What our people long for in the Abrahamic covenant is unconditionally promised by grace and mercy—but only by grace and mercy, since our disobedience warrants only a curse. It is this grace and mercy that the *torah* of Moses compels us to seek, even in the greater seed of Abraham, Messiah Yeshua.

The blessings of God through the Mosaic covenant were based upon our obedience, but the covenant was broken by our disobedience (Exodus 32). Like the Noahic covenant (Isaiah 24:5), the Mosaic was everlasting, but also breakable. God "was a husband to them," in that he kept His promises; God kept His word, even if we failed. Our failure necessitates the need for grace in Messiah. Before my father of blessed memory passed on, I had a chance to share Messiah with him. His response was, "Sam, I'm not good enough." I pleaded with him "That's why we need Messiah, Dad!" My dad understood the truth of Moses; we all have sinned and no one deserves a blessing, especially not the greatest blessing of all. The law of Moses shows us our need for the atonement, forgiveness and new life in Yeshua, as detailed in the New Covenant.

NEW AND MOSAIC COVENANTS COMPARED

How is this New Covenant different? Unlike the Mosaic the New Covenant is unbreakable because it's unconditional. It's not conditioned on our obedience to keep it, but upon God's ability to keep us. In Jeremiah 31:31-34, God reiterated seven times what *He* will do:

1. "*I* will make a new covenant" (31);
2. "*I* will make ... with the house of Israel" (33);
3. "*I* will put My law within them" (33);

4. "On their heart *I* will write it" (33);
5. "*I* will be their God" (33);
6. "*I* will forgive their iniquity" (34);
7. "Their sin *I* will remember no more" (34).

The New Covenant is based upon what God Himself will accomplish. The guarantee is one-sided—not based on our faithfulness, but on His grace. As Jonah declared, "salvation is from the Lord" (Jonah 3:9). It is a work of God alone, completely based on His ability and faithfulness. This power of God for salvation is also His enablement through the New Covenant to follow Him.

> Not that we are adequate in ourselves to consider anything as coming from ourselves, but our adequacy is from God, who made us adequate servants of a New Covenant. (2 Corinthians 3:5-6)

God saves and keeps us, even the Mosaic Covenant reveals we need both saving and keeping.

The covenants are also different in their content, as three aspects will show. *First, while the New is a covenant that removes all remembrance of sin* (Jeremiah 31:34), the Mosaic Covenant had a yearly reminder of sin and a perpetual priesthood (Leviticus 16). The priests' job was never done.

Second, in the New Covenant, Messiah combines in his person the offices of king and priest. Zechariah prophesied of a high priest that would be given a crown, saying:

> Thus says the Lord of hosts, "Behold, a man whose name is Branch, for he will branch out from where he is; and he will build the temple of the Lord. Yes, it is he who will build the temple of the Lord, and he who will bear the honor and sit and rule on his throne. Thus, he will be a priest on his throne, and the counsel of peace will be between the two offices." (Zechariah 6:12-14; for more on "Branch" as Messianic, see also Isaiah 4:2; Jeremiah 23:5-6; Zechariah 3:8)

Here, the priesthood and the kingship will be combined in one person. But this could not occur under the Mosaic Covenant. Only Aaron's descendants were permitted to be high priests under the Mosaic Covenant, whereas, based on God's promises to David, only a descendant of his is rightfully considered king (2 Samuel 7:12-14; cf. Zechariah 6:12-13). For these two offices to be combined would require a different covenant. David himself prophesied that the one Messiah would be a king and also a priest (Psalm 110:1-2; 4). However, His priesthood would not be of Aaron: "The Lord has sworn and will not change His mind, You are a priest forever according to the order of Melchizedek." The writer of Hebrews points to this passage as an argument that the New Covenant is a different covenant:

> Now if perfection was through the Levitical priesthood (for on the basis of it the people received the Law), what further need was there for another priest to arise according to the order of Melchizedek, and not be designated according to the order of Aaron? For when the priesthood is changed, of necessity there takes place a change of law also. For the one concerning whom these things are spoken belongs to another tribe, from which no one has officiated at the altar. For it is evident that our Lord was descended from Judah, a tribe with reference to which Moses spoke nothing concerning priests. (Hebrews 7:11-14)

The New Covenant, by necessity of the work of the Messiah as the priest-king, must be different than the Mosaic. Some have pushed back saying that only part of the Mosaic stipulations were changed at Messiah's coming. Though one writer acknowledges the logical necessity of such change in light of Messiah's work, he argues that the change applies only to the priesthood and the sacrificial system, leaving the other parts identical. This means, for him, interpreting "change" (*metathesis*) as a "retention of the basic structure of the *torah*, with some of its elements rearranged" (Hebrews 7:12; Stern,

JNTC, 681). Yet it is not strong enough to read the "change" (*metathesis*) of law in Hebrews 7:12 merely as modification or rearrangement, just as Enoch was taken up he was removed (*metathesis*), not partially, but completely (Hebrews 11:5, 27; Genesis 5:24). In reality, the moral, legal, and ceremonial aspects of the *torah* from the Mount Sinai covenant should not be considered independent parts, but rather one unit (Jacob 2:10-11). Rather than making internal modifications to the *torah* of that covenant, the New Covenant is a completely different entity.

Third, in the New Covenant God promises a place in the temple for the foreigners and eunuchs who join themselves to the Lord (Isaiah 56:3-7). However, under the Mosaic Covenant eunuchs were excluded from the Temple:

> No one who is emasculated or has his male organ cut off shall enter the assembly of the Lord. (Deuteronomy 23:1)

Had the New Covenant been the same as the First Covenant, the Gentiles discussed in Acts 15 would need to be circumcised to become partakers of the promises of the New Covenant. Yet in Acts 15, we see that these Gentiles were accepted as Gentiles, who were not obligated to keep the Mosaic stipulations. By definition the Body of Messiah is a table fellowship of Jews and Gentiles in Yeshua, and this table of fellowship (better known as the Lord's Supper) would be prohibited under the Mosaic covenant.

Therefore, in the New Covenant is a security that the Mosaic could never provide.

> Therefore He is able also to save forever those who draw near to God through Him, since He always lives to make intercession for them. (Hebrews 7:25)

It is not that the first covenant (called first because it was the first made with Israel) was, or is, evil. May it never be! No, the problem is not the agreement, but our failure to keep it.

Thus, the Mosaic served as preparatory for the New Covenant (Galatians 3:24; Romans 3:21), but couldn't accomplish God's ultimate purpose to save souls. Like a mirror it could show the blemish, but could not heal it; like a thermometer it can accurately tell you how cold the room is, but cannot heat it up. The New Covenant is not a restored or a renewed Mosaic covenant, but is new, different, and better!

God wants to do something radically different through the New Covenant for our people and all people who will believe on Messiah. This idea of "new" becomes a theme of this covenant.

> If anyone is in Messiah, he is a new creature; the old things passed away; behold, new things have come. (2 Corinthians 5:17)

This is the fulfillment of what Ezekiel foresaw as "a new heart" and "a new Spirit;" in fact it is "His own Spirit," that is, God the Holy Spirit (Ezekiel 26:26-27).

In Messiah and His New Covenant we have His peace with HaShem and each other, Jew and Gentile together. This is the fulfillment of the Abrahamic Covenant that brings the blessing of the seed of Abraham to all nations (Genesis 12:3): "He is our Peace… that in Himself He might make the two into one new man, establishing peace" (Ephesians 2:15). This is a new unity that is not based on ethnicity, but the Spirit.

> Neither is circumcision anything, nor uncircumcision, but a new creation." (Galatians 6:15)

Yes, it is radically different, so that we are prepared for a new heaven, new earth, and the new Jerusalem predicted by Isaiah and John (Isaiah 65:17-18; Revelation 21:1-2).

In Messiah, we are under a New Covenant, and this newness is seen in its key differences. This is true though all covenants are all eternally established, or *olam*. In the next chapter, we will look further at the differences and continuities as we consider the provisions of this New Covenant.

Oh let Israel say,
"His lovingkindness is everlasting."
Psalm 118:2

12

NEW COVENANT PROVISIONS

> "But this is the covenant which I will make with the house of Israel after those days," declares the LORD, "I will put My law within them and on their heart I will write it; and I will be their God, and they shall be My people."
> Jeremiah 31:33

As we have been considering the New Covenant, one phrase will help us keep in mind the continuity of the Jewish people. Jeremiah writes in 31:33 that this covenant is with "the house of Israel." Yet two verses earlier, God said that He would make it with "the house of Israel and the house of Judah." So, what happened to Judah in 31:33?

After the reign of Solomon (c. 950 BCE), and at the time of Jeremiah (600 BCE), the house of Israel had been divided in to two kingdoms: the northern nation maintained the name Israel, also called Ephraim, after the largest tribe in that area. The southern nation took on the name of the predominant tribe in that area, Judah. There were constant wars between them until the northern tribe was conquered by Assyria and went into Assyrian exile in 712 BCE. Judah remained until they were conquered by Babylon, and went into Babylonian captivity in 606 BCE.

Today there are some who think that the northern country of Israel became "the lost tribes." Various groups have alleged that these lost tribes were dispersed into Europe and Asia and eventually became Christians through Paul's mission. These believers in Messiah, who became the core of Christians, are alleged to be Israel (or "Ephraim").

Yet, Ezra and Nehemiah are clear that all the tribes of Israel returned after the Babylonian captivity under Zerubbabel. Those who returned are called "the people of Israel" (Ezra 2:2), and the sacrifices were made for the nation as a whole "according to the number of the tribes of Israel" (Ezra 6:17; 8:35). The idea of "lost tribes" was not known to the prophet Zechariah, for in his prophecy he speaks of "all the tribes of Israel" (Zechariah 9:1). Nor did the New Covenant writers know of any tribes being lost. Luke wrote, "there was a prophetess, Anna the daughter of Phanuel, of the tribe of Asher" (Luke 2:36), though the tribe of Asher being one of the alleged lost tribes. Jacob writes as well: "to the twelve tribes who are dispersed abroad" (Jacob 1:1). Paul knew of no lost tribes, but only of "the promise to which our twelve tribes hope to attain, as they earnestly serve God night and day" (Acts 26:7).

This is why Jeremiah says that Judah and Israel are "the house of Israel" in verse 33, for the people of Israel (the Jewish people) are one, and the promised covenant is theirs. God says, "I will make this covenant with the house of Israel"—and He will!

Jeremiah envisions this taking place "after those days," when Israel will nationally accept the New Covenant. As we considered briefly in chapter 1, this phrase that characterizes this whole section of Jeremiah (30:3, 24; 31:27, 29, 31). This revival of national Israel comes after the days "of wrath" (Jeremiah 30:24-31:1; Zechariah 13:9), which is called "the time of Jacob's trouble" at the end of this age (Jeremiah 30:7; Ezekiel 37:23-27). The recipients of this covenant are, in fact, the Jewish people, but may be applied by faith to anyone who trusts in the Messiah of Israel (Matthew 26:28; Luke 22:20; Hebrews 12:22-24).

In this covenant we see three gracious provisions, each connected to one another by "and":

1. "I will put My law within them and on their heart I will write it" (Jeremiah 31:33).
2. "And I will be their God, and they shall be My people" (Jeremiah 31:33).
3. "And they will not teach again, each man his neighbor and each man his brother, saying, 'Know the Lord,' for they will all know Me, from the least of them to the greatest of them" (Jeremiah 31:34).

Their connection to each other is one of dependence. Some have wanted to skip to the final state—universal knowledge of God wherein everyone relates to God in perfect harmony. Yet verse 34 is a separate sentence and shows the results of the preceding provisions. Those who have had God's *torah* written on the hearts, are thereby in relationship with God, and "know the Lord" (Jeremiah 31:34).

First: Internal Provision of the Truth of God

As a prophetic development of "the circumcision of the heart" that Moses first spoke of in Deuteronomy 30:6, we are not surprised to see where, according to Jeremiah, God's work for a New Covenant will be accomplished: "on their heart I will write it." God wants to have the truth where it has the most impact: on your heart! The emphasis of Scripture is that it is written on hearts and not on stones. The "new heart" of Ezekiel is a "circumcised heart" of Moses by "the work of Messiah" in order that the New Covenant will be lived out (Ezekiel 36:26; Colossians 2:11-13). Messiah's teaching emphasized the heart because the truth needs to be internalized before it can be externalized (Matthew 5:28; 6:21; Mark 7:21). The eternal relationship with God begins as an internal work of God in our hearts. Please note that God states "I will put My law (*torah*) within them." What God writes on our heart is "law," or *torah*. The word *torah* comes from the Hebrew root (*yarah*) "to throw," "cast," or "point out" (Genesis 46:28; Exodus 15:4). Thus it means "instruction" or "teaching" (Psalm 78:1), and often translated "law" because God's instruction is authoritative, not merely a suggestion. However, must *torah* here refer to the Law of Moses specifically? No, not at all.

We must remember that the word *torah* (instruction) is used quite generally throughout the *Tanakh*. Therefore, Moses gave *torah* "pre-Sinai," that is, before the Ten Commandments and Sinai *torah* were given (Exodus 16:4, 28). It is used as single law or principle: "The same law (*torah*) shall apply to the native as to the stranger who sojourns among you" (Exodus 12:49). *Torah* also refers to the teaching of a parent, the wise, and a wise wife (Proverbs 1:8; 4:2; 13:14; 31:26). Now, Jeremiah 31:33 clearly refers to divine instruction ("my *torah*"), but it is the divine instructions of the New Covenant.

A bumper sticker read: "When all else fails, lower your standards." Unfortunately, many people think the New Covenant functions this way, lowering the standards on morality, holiness, godliness and righteousness. This is not the case at all (Matthew 5:17-20). With the establishment of the New Covenant, its recipients have divine instruction placed on our hearts, guiding us to live in Messiah Yeshua, according to God's character. Let's first understand the relationship between law and covenant in general.

Logically, covenant precedes law. Covenant establishes the relationship; *torah* is the instruction showing how the covenant relationship is lived out. *Torah* was given only to the people in a covenant relationship with God. This is the case of the covenants with Adam, Noah, and Abraham (Hosea 6:7; Genesis 9:9; Genesis 26:5). Law is God's governance through

His covenant relationship with His people. All *torah* is given in regards to how we are to relate to God, and thus it actually precedes human sin (Genesis 2:16-17; 3:7). Law and covenant can parallel one another, since they are so closely tied together, such that to break one is to break the other (Psalm 78:10). If you break covenant it is because you broke a law of that covenant; if you break a law, then, assuming the covenant was breakable, you have broken covenant as well (Jeremiah 31:32).

All *torah* or instruction is determined by the specific covenant context, functioning as the stipulations of any particular covenant. Hence, a new covenant means new *torah*; there are no "*torah*-free" covenants. The *torah* is necessarily different, even as the covenant context is different.

Therefore, the complaint that "without being under the authority of Mosaic Law, believers would be lawless" overlooks the fact that as Messianic believers we are under Messianic *torah* (1 Corinthians 9:21; Galatians 6:12; Romans 8:4). We are not permitted to be lawless, but are called to holiness (1 Peter 1:15).

Since all biblical covenants are from HaShem we would expect their instruction to have similarities as well as differences. One might naturally wonder, "What are the differences between the Mosaic *torah* in the Covenant from Mt. Sinai, and the Messianic *torah* in the New Covenant?"

In the New Covenant, marriages are to be unbreakable and permanent. We do not break our word. This is clearly seen in Matthew 19:3-11. In this section some of the traditional religious leaders asked Yeshua about His position on marriage, divorce, and remarriage (Matthew 19:3). Some rabbis at that time taught that a man could divorce his wife for almost any reason; others, though, were more stringent on the matter. In his response, Yeshua brought them back to the original intent of marriage as Moses wrote it in Genesis 1:27 and 2:24, concluding, "So they are no longer two, but one flesh. What therefore God has joined together let no man separate" (Matthew 19:6). The

167

implication is that the couple is to stay married, and not even to think of themselves as two, but as one.

Yeshua's interlocutors objected to His teaching since it didn't square up with the Mosaic stipulations (Deuteronomy 24:1-4). They said to Him, "Why then did Moses command to give a certificate of divorce, and to put her away?"

Yeshua's response highlighted the fact that something new had come along. He said to them,

> Because of your hardness of heart Moses permitted you to divorce your wives; but from the beginning it has not been this way. And I say to you, whoever divorces his wife, except for immorality and marries another woman, commits adultery. (Matthew 19:8-9)

The reason for the divorce was "hardness of heart" and that is why Moses permitted a certificate of divorce. It is also why Moses and Jeremiah wrote that we need a heart circumcision (Deuteronomy 10:16; Jeremiah 4:4). Divorce regulations arose because of hardness of heart. However, Moses' hope for marriage would be fulfilled in the New Covenant as he understood it (Deuteronomy 30:6).

The problem of the broken marriage is sin: not incompatibility, or irreconcilable differences, or "we've grown apart"— but sin. Since Messiah has come, Moses' certificate of divorce is no longer necessary: the "hardness of heart" problem has been remedied. Therefore, "hardness of heart" is no longer a valid reason for divorce in the New Covenant. If you divorce for reasons other than (serial) "adultery" (Matthew 19:9; 5:32), you must either reconcile with your spouse, or stay single (1 Corinthians 7:10-13).

Messiah's New Covenant *torah* makes divorce much more difficult to obtain than the *torah* of Moses. If you're looking for a "quickie" divorce, non-Messianic Judaism today is much more amenable to this idea than Messiah is. The stringency of Messiah's teaching shocked His disciples, such that they thought it better not to marry at all rather than try and live with just one person for your whole life (Matthew 19:10)! Messiah lets them know that staying single is for those that are gifted to do so (Matthew 19:11), though of course marriage is the natural norm.

Matters such as prohibitions against incest are not specifically restated in New Covenant texts. Thus, some have argued that without Mosaic authority, we have insufficient guidance from the New Covenant. However, in the New Covenant we are completely restricted from all forms of immorality, not only in deed, but in thought as well. The Greek word that is used meaning immorality is *porneia*, and covers the whole range of immoral behaviors from internet porn to incest, from immoral daydreams to homosexuality. The New Covenant covers all immoral issues without necessarily detailing each one (though lists are given in Romans 1:28-30, 1 Corinthians 6:9-10). Realistically, Messiah's teaching should be enough to convict everyone, in that it went to the root of the problem:

> But I say to you, that everyone who looks at a woman with lust for her has already committed adultery with her in his heart. If your right eye makes you stumble, tear it out and throw it from you; for it is better for you to lose one of the parts of your body, then for your whole body to be thrown into Hell. (Matthew 5:28-29)

That's a pretty stern warning. Yes, there is forgiveness for all sins in Messiah's atonement (1 John 1:7, 9). However, this does not make sin somehow less evil, or less deserving of punishment for believers than it is for unbelievers. The New Covenant gives severe warning to believers who fool around with sin and presumptuously think that God will overlook such matters. They will be chastened severely, possibly to the point of losing their physical lives (1 Corinthians 10:5-11; 11:30; Jacob 5:20, Revelation 2:5, 16, 22, 3:3, etc.). We are to wage war against our own lusts, anger, and pride, and we have the divine resource in the battle!

In general, when we think about the *torah* of Messiah we see three types:

1. **The *torah* of Messiah which is commanded.** These commands are clear imperatives that direct behavior, beliefs and attitudes in godliness and love. Commands regarding our love and care for one another, as well as the matters we just considered, are included in this area. Interestingly, in Messianic *torah*, there are commands which differentiate between Jews and Gentiles: the latter are commanded not to seek circumcision, and the former are commanded not to seek uncircumcision.

2. **The *torah* of Messiah which is modeled.** These behaviors of the Messiah and his disciples described in Scriptures that demonstrate godliness and love, but are not given in commandment form. By touching a leper, Yeshua demonstrates love, but of course there is no commandment to touch lepers; Paul is bitten by a snake, but there is no commandment to handle snakes; Yeshua died on a cross, but gives no commandment to die on crosses. These provide models for how to walk with Messiah.

3. **The *torah* of Messiah that is principled.** These instructions on various issues were meant to give wisdom on the application of love, faith and hope, but were never given as imperatives. These include cover topics like not eating meat so as not to stumble a weaker brother; not accepting pay as a minister, so as not to hinder the Good News; and not dining in a pagan temple so as not to dishonor the Lord. The basic issue is that eternal love limits personal liberty.

We do not teach contrary to Moses, but rather seek to understand how its wisdom flowers into New Covenant fulfillment. This is a subtle issue and can lead to misunderstanding, for even Paul was misunderstood, and was accused of teaching Jewish believers to abandon Moses (Acts 21:21-24; 2 Peter 3:16). But isn't the New Covenant more lenient on certain matters? Let's look and see.

THE NEW COVENANT AND FOOD LAWS (KASHRUT)

Since the New Covenant is actually "new," not merely a renewal of the Mosaic Torah, there should not be a surprise if a number of external issues now have changed priority. In regard to matters of food and drink, it may at first glance appear that the New Covenant removes dietary laws (*kashrut*) altogether as a moral issue for the New Covenant believer. Yet the truth is more complex. Since we are not permitted to use our liberty selfishly, but to care for others, it might well be said that all issues have become "moral issues" in Messiah.

Kashrut literally means what is "fit" or "proper," and is used to refer to the Mosaic regulations given over eating, and also to their refinement and application through rabbinic interpretation. Throughout history, there has been much speculation and research on the general health and sanitary advantages of a kosher diet. For example, the Talmud states that "the mouth of a swine is as dirty as dung itself" (Berachot 25a). However, in Mosaic Law, the purpose we see laid out for the dietary laws was spiritual holiness, or setting apart the Jewish people from the nations (Exodus 22:31; Leviticus 11:44-45; Deuteronomy 14:21). Though Maimonides, as a physician, considers the health aspects when looking at the command "not to boil a young goat in the milk of its mother," he granted it was "most probably also prohibited because it is somehow connected with idolatry. Perhaps it was part of the ritual of certain pagan festivals" (Exodus 23:19; *Guide to the Perplexed*, 3:48). These rituals would have been observed by peoples within the land which Israel was commanded to shun.

By the time of the New Covenant writings, the prohibited foods did not necessarily have the same religious significance in the land of Israel. If separation from local pagan worship was at least some of the reason for the dietary laws, then it is understandable why New Covenant *torah* does not give the same emphasis to *kashrut*.

The problem, however, has been to assume that because Messianic *torah* does not prohibit particular foods, one is therefore permitted to eat them. While in Mosaic *torah*, *kashrut* was a matter of command, in Messianic *torah*, it is a matter for wisdom. In 1 Corinthians 8:13 Paul says that if meat causes his brother to stumble, "I will never eat meat again." The issue is not a command about meat, but the detrimental effect such a situation could have upon another. For the follower of Messiah, love limits liberty.

Paul goes on to teach that because of his concern for the spiritual state of his people, he would go "under the (Mosaic) law." Thus, in Paul's desire to be a faithful follower of Messiah, he would have never eaten unkosher foods if it detracted from the truth. His example presents good reasons for Jewish believers (and all believers) to take their diet seriously as a matter of faithfulness to the God of Israel. Do we assume "do whatever you want" as the rule for food practices among Jewish and Gentile believers alike? Is it not possible to imply, through indifference towards *kashrut,* that God is indifferent towards the Jewish people? When believing groups serve pork at their breakfasts (as does happen), for example, we imply that unless a traditional Jewish person is willing to change his faithful eating habits, then he is not welcome. Is that Christian liberty?

On the other hand, *kashrut* must not be legislated as a basis for fellowship either. In 1 Timothy 4:1-5, Paul warns believers against getting involved with "doctrines of demons" being promoted by false teachers in their area. Though that phrase "doctrine of demons" sounds very serious, it refers in particular to forbidding marriage and "abstaining from foods which God has created to be gratefully shared in by those who believe and know the truth" (1 Timothy 4:3).

Paul goes to explain why: "for everything created by God is good, and nothing is to be rejected if it is received with gratitude" (1 Timothy 4:4). On this verse, some have said that in fact *kashrut* must be abolished completely (that we should enforce liberty, so to speak). However, Paul is talking about pagan asceticism here, and his reasoning continues: "for it is sanctified by means of the word of God and prayer." Since *kashrut* was obviously a matter of "the word of God," it is unwise to base a sweeping rejection of food laws on this verse.

Marriage and food matters at first may not seem like demonic issues, but Paul's point is simple. Those who promoted these practices were treating them as a basis for walking with God. However, anything other than Messiah which becomes the focus of our attention for godliness is a demonic diversion, a doctrine of demons. It is "the little foxes that spoil the vines" (Song of Solomon 2:15). Messiah alone is our redemption and hope. Regarding the "mystery of godliness," Yeshua is our "common confession," not food laws (1 Timothy 3:16). In the New Covenant, it is Messiah's one sacrifice that is needed for your salvation and sanctification, for eternity. As it is written: "we have been sanctified through the offering of the body of Messiah Yeshua once for all" (Hebrews 10:10).

Food issues were given as a matter of identifying Jewish people as a peculiar people. But they are not to become sanctification issues: we are neither better for eating, nor worse for abstaining, or even fasting. Regarding fasting, if a person leads others to believe he is fasting while he eats in secret, he is deceiving those who may think him to be a godly person. However, if he really does fast, but begins to admire himself for doing so, thinking, "wow, I am really holy," he is deceiving himself, and *self*-deception is even worse.

If we think that keeping *kashrut* makes us more godly or sanctified, then we have elevated matters of food over Messiah. If we are more concerned for other people and Messiah's testimony than how free or unfree we are to eat, we are moving in the right direction; this is a sign of spiritual maturity and a closer walk with the Lord. Rather than permitting certain foods or making abstention a basis for fellowship, we seek to prioritize what is prioritized by New Covenant *torah*.

Romans 14 and 15 speak to Jewish and Gentile relations (in chapter 9 of this book we considered the end of the Romans portion). Those who were concerned with the meat being offered to idols would eat only vegetables so as to keep from ceremonial defilement by unkosher food. In other words, they went on the "Daniel diet" (see Daniel 1). Paul did not correct these so-called "weaker brethren." Rather, he told the so-called strong and weak to "accept one another" (Romans 14:1-3) and not to "stumble" one another (Romans 14:13-16). Those who thought they were strong were to bear the weakness of the weak (Romans 15:1-3).

Why wouldn't Paul tell the weak to just get over their religious hang-ups, and eat the meat? Or, why not tell the strong to be more careful about what they ate? Though he did say "let each be convinced in his own mind," he did not take the opportunity to prescribe a biblical menu for either group. Rather than attempt to correct eating habits, Paul re-prioritized their focus, "for the kingdom of God is not eating and drinking, but righteousness and peace and joy in the Holy Spirit" (Romans 14:17). Once more, the food is not the issue, but how we treat each other is.

In Colossians 2:9-17, Paul again states that because of who Yeshua is (the fullness of deity incarnate), we are not to judge each other by what we "eat or drink" (Colossians 2:16), since all these matters, as well as the various days of observance, are foreshadowing of Messiah (Colossians 2:17). The real issue for all Messianic believers is not eating or drinking, or how to celebrate the holidays, but how we love our neighbor as ourselves. Do we exalt Yeshua in every area of life?

Messiah called Peter to preach the Good News to all nations (Matthew 28:19). But Peter was having a hard time fulfilling the call, because all of those nations were filled with Gentiles. Thus God had to give Peter a vision so he would know it is perfectly proper to minister to and mix with the *goyim*. Peter had a vision in which he saw a sheet filled with unkosher food.

Then God said, "Rise, Peter; kill and eat." "But Peter said, "By no means, Lord, for I have never eaten anything unholy and unclean." (Acts 10:13-14)

It's hard to put "no" and "Lord" in the same sentence, but Peter did it. Now, the point of the vision was not literally to put swine on the menu, but to admonish Peter to show hospitality toward the Gentiles, "that I should not call any man unholy or unclean" (Acts 10:28). Just as Peter had never eaten unkosher food, by that same token, he had never eaten with Gentiles. Later he would be called out for being inconsistent in his fellowship with Gentile believers (Galatians 2:11-12). The inconsistency was not that he ate unkosher food, nor was it that he ate kosher food, but that he disregarded fellowship with non-Jews. His specific eating habits were simply not in question.

Regarding the Temple, its sacrifices for sin and its regulations, Hebrews says they are:

> Accordingly both gifts and sacrifices are offered which cannot make the worshiper perfect in conscience, since they relate only to food and drink and various washings, regulations for the body imposed until a time of reformation. (Hebrews 9:9-10)

There is some discussion about the meaning of these "food and drink" regulations imposed until the "time of reformation" — literally, "time of straightening out." It may refer to *kashrut* (Leviticus 11), whereas others have referred it to the laws for what priests could eat in the Holy Place (Exodus 29:31-33). It could also refer to the food and drink eaten by Israel during the feasts (Leviticus 23). In light of the truth of the priesthood of all believers (1 Peter 2:9), I take "food and drink" in principle to refer to all of the above, since they are "regulations for the body" or external issues (literally "fleshly regulations"). These regulations were not able to internally "straighten" us out, but show us our desperate need for straightening, which Messiah has fully accomplished. They were not authoritative in their jurisdiction over a believer forever, but until Yeshua came with the "new order" (Romans 7:1-6; Galatians 3:19-24).

The writer of Hebrews also tells us "it is good for the heart to be strengthened by grace, not by foods, through which those who were so occupied were not benefited" (Hebrews 13:9). The point is not that kosher food is somehow an unhealthy or unbeneficial diet— not at all! It is just that kosher food, as healthy as it may be, as good as it may be as a matter of testimony, does not "strengthen" or "benefit" the inner person; foods do not in and of themselves help us spiritually. It is God's grace in Messiah that is our full benefit and power from on high. Thus, "food will not commend us to God; we are neither the worse if we do not eat, nor the better if we do eat" (1 Corinthians 8:8).

In context, we must remember that Paul was not only speaking of unkosher foods, but of food that was corrupted by pagan idolatry and the very food which Daniel refused to eat; such food is strictly forbidden in the New Covenant (Acts 15:20, 29; 21:25; Revelation 2:14, 20). Pagan practices did not only include eating food offered to idols but also the asceticism of "do not handle, do not taste, do not touch... in accordance with the commandments and teachings of men" (Colossians 2:21-22; cf. 1 Timothy 4:1-5). Unlike *kashrut*, the pagan ascetic regulations were from man and not God. Yet Paul is clear that the food has no spiritual value *or* harm in and of itself. Why is the food forbidden then? In Acts 15:20-21, it was prohibited because of its detrimental affect to communicating the Good News on the local Jewish community; in Corinth, there was the additional issue of stumbling weaker brethren who came out of pagan lifestyle (1 Corinthians 8:7-12). Paul declares about his liberty: "Therefore, if food causes my brother to stumble, I will never eat meat again, so that I will not cause my brother to stumble" (1 Corinthians 8:13). His liberty was to *not* eat for the sake of others.

In general, liberty is given to edify the least, evangelize the lost, and exalt the Lord; never for self-centered desires. Where there is liberty in our menu, we also limit our liberty out of love, and are sure never to allow our liberty to cause a weaker believer to stumble (1 Corinthians 8); to never allow our liberty to hinder the Good News to unsaved people (1 Corinthians 9); and to never allow our liberty to dishonor the Lord (1 Corinthians 10).

In this regard I have not found keeping a kosher diet to be a hindrance to the communication of the Good News, nor has keeping *kashrut* stumbled any believer – though it might if I was to make acceptance of that diet a basis for fellowship. Liberty is given to do God's will and help us to be more effective in our calling, especially as it refers to the Jewish people. The issue of what I eat is always secondary to advancing God's agenda for the salvation of Israel, for the edification of other believers, and for the honor of the King and His kingdom (Romans 14:17).

SHABBAT IN NEW COVENANT TORAH

A popular idea is that the seventh-day Sabbath (Saturday) has been replaced in the New Covenant by a Sunday Sabbath. Yet another idea is that Sunday, while not literally the "new Sabbath," quickly became the normative day for believers to gather in worship after Messiah's resurrection. Of course, without being too clever, we should note that the earliest believers in Yeshua worshipped everyday (Acts 2:46). Even so, this was always done in a Jewish frame of reference, and regularly on the Temple grounds. We are strongly exhorted to "not forsake the assembling together as is the habit of some" (Hebrews 10:25). But when should we forsake not, Saturday or Sunday? This question has generated a conundrum and a controversy. On the one hand, it is true that, unlike the other nine of the Ten Commandments, the obligation to keep the Sabbath is not repeated in the New Covenant Scriptures. The closest mention is found in Hebrews 4:9, "for there remains a Sabbath rest for the people of God." The word used here *sabbatismos,* or "Sabbath rest," is formed from the verb to "keep sabbath" (Exodus 16:30; 2 Chronicles 36:21). It is possible that the writer to the Hebrews is indicating that keeping Shabbat itself focuses us on the rest that God gives in Messiah. More likely, the writer of Hebrews is saying that all believers find their true Shabbat rest by faith in Yeshua. This text does not actually obligate Sabbath observance.

On the other hand, in the New Covenant, no other day for communal worship is specified, including Sunday. What is abundantly clear, moreover, is that believers did observe and continue to worship on Shabbat (Luke 23:56; Acts 13:14; 16:13; 17:2; 18:4).

As "the Lord of the Sabbath," not only is Messiah authoritative of how it is to be observed, but ultimately the day speaks of Him, and our rest in Him:

> Come to Me, all who are weary and heavy-laden, and I will give you rest. Take My yoke upon you, and learn from Me, for I am gentle and humble in heart; and you shall find rest for your souls. (Matthew 11:28-29)

God established Shabbat as a special, identifying sign between Him and His people Israel (Exodus 31:12-13; see also Ezekiel 20:20). In light of this, it is wise for Messianic believers to worship together on Shabbat as a testimony to His Lordship, as well as our identification with Israel. As a matter of example and wisdom, in other words, we use our liberty in assembling together to best testify that Yeshua is the "Lord of the Sabbath" (Matthew 12:8). In 'keeping Shabbat,' we are to keep it unto Messiah: we are to demonstrate compassion (Matthew 12:7), and do good for others (Matthew 12:12), which may include all manner of good deeds (John 5:9-11). On Shabbat, as we reorient our lives around God, we testify to His goodness and grace in Yeshua.

In the New Covenant Scriptures, the places that allude to Sunday do not indicate a normative day for corporate worship.

The phrase *"the first day of the week"* is used eight times, of which six refer to the day of resurrection (Matthew 28:1; Mark 16:2, 9; Luke 24:1; John 20:1, 19). The other two are taken by some to refer to occasions of worship and fellowship (Acts 20:7, 1 Corinthians 16:2). This first day of the week has been tied to "the Lord's Day" in Revelation 1:10 by church tradition.

In Matthew 28:1 we read, "Now after the Sabbath, as it began to dawn toward the first day of the week, Mary Magdalene and the other Mary came to look at the grave." In other words, when Matthew wrote his account of Messiah (circa 60-70 CE), the seventh day as such was still the Sabbath, and was thus distinguished from "the first day of the week."

In Acts 20:6, we read, "and we sailed from Philippi after the days of Unleavened Bread…". It seems Luke is careful to indicate that Paul kept *Pesach* (Passover) with the brethren in Philippi, and only traveled after the feast days were concluded. In the following verse, it appears that Paul and his team had stayed there through Shabbat:

> …and came to them at Troas within five days; and there we stayed seven days. And on the first day of the week, when we were gathered together to break bread, Paul began talking to them, intending to depart the next day, and he prolonged his message until midnight. (Acts 20:7)

In the customary order, each day begins at sundown: "And there was evening and there was morning, one day" (Genesis 1:5). Thus in Acts 20:7, the first day of the week more likely meant Saturday evening, at the beginning of the day. This would have coincided with a weekly event called a *havdalah* service, recognizing the end of Shabbat on Saturday evening. The *havdalah* service usually consisted of prayers, candle lighting, breaking of bread and fellowship, and would have been a convenient time for Paul to teach. So, in Acts 20, since Paul's intention was to leave the next day, he took the occasion to extend his evening message until midnight.

Paul had set his schedule to get to Jerusalem before Shavuot, or Pentecost (Acts 20:16). Once more, Luke indicates his own Messianic discipleship under Paul, in a setting where the feast days were touchstones in the lives of first century believers. As these events are seen in a Messianic Jewish frame of reference and emphasis, it should appear strange to read corporate Sunday worship into the setting of Acts 20:7.

In 1 Corinthians 16:1-4 Paul gives instruction on the collection for the poor to be taken to Jerusalem. Each person was to set aside money on the first day of the week (1 Corinthians 16:2). Again, it is remarkable how some have read a Sunday worship tradition into this verse. From a Jewish frame of reference, on the Sabbath, observant Jewish people do not handle nor carry money, nor do they give or receive money (*Kitzur Shulchan Aruch* 89:3). Mainstream Christian commentaries widely recognize this lack of reference to corporate worship. F.F. Bruce acknowledges, "it is doubtful whether there is any liturgical significance in this mention of the first day of every week ... nor were the individual sums to be taken to the church and handed over to the community treasurer" (*1 and 2 Corinthians*, p. 158). Leon Morris likewise takes it to mean that "each one is to keep the money in store at home" (*First Corinthians*, p. 238). John Ruef is quite clear:

> There is no evidence here that this putting-aside had anything to do with a worship service on Sunday. It sounds more like a practical means of making sure that some kind of contribution would be there when Paul arrived... It is simply easier for people of modest means to give a number of small contributions over an extended period of time than to give a relatively large sum all at once (*Paul's First Letter to Corinth*, 181).

If the money collection had nothing to do with worship services, this is because the custom of New Covenant worship was normatively tied to the seventh-day Shabbat. Make no mistake: it is true that New Covenant believers have the liberty to worship the Lord any and every day, and to live a life of 'Shabbat rest' in Messiah through every activity of their lives. Also, there is nothing wrong with taking Sunday to celebrate the resurrection of Messiah. However, when our *organizing principle* has been the explicit or implicit assumption that the day has been "transferred," this has wrought confusion and division for the Body of Messiah. This error distances faith in Messiah from its Jewishness, provides yet another stumbling block for our people to consider Yeshua as the Messiah, and stands against the Gentile's calling to make Israel jealous. We must not abuse our liberty in Messiah.

OY! CIRCUMCISION & GENTILES

Circumcision is the sign of the (unconditional) Abrahamic covenant, and as such, it remains a testimony kept by Jewish believers. This is seen in the example of Timothy, who was circumcised by Paul, and in the command for Jews not to seek to be uncircumcised (Acts 16:1-3; 1 Corinthians 7:18). Yet, Jews and Gentiles are differentiated on this matter. In fact, an important distinction between the Mosaic and the Messianic *torah* is the role Gentiles have as Gentiles. The law of Moses says,

> but if a stranger sojourns with you, and celebrates the Passover to the Lord, let all his males be circumcised, and then let him come near to celebrate it; and he shall be like a native of the land. But no uncircumcised person may eat of it. (Exodus 12:48)

This was not trivial or irrelevant to the early believers, especially to Gentiles. They understood that Mosaic *torah* forbids Gentiles to participate in Passover without first being circumcised. Yet under New Covenant authority, circumcision is not required to participate (1 Corinthians 5:8); and in fact, Gentiles are called not to seek circumcision whatsoever (1 Corinthians 7:18).

Similarly, as we saw, having fellowship and eating in a Gentile home was cause enough for Peter to be called out to answer for this apparent offense (Acts 11:3). Gentile fellowship was also the issue which Paul confronted Peter about in Galatians 2:11-14. When some of the circumcision faction from Jerusalem came to Antioch, Peter bailed on his Gentile brothers to please the faction of the circumcision. Of all people, Peter should have known better. It was Peter whom God first used to open the door for Gentiles! They now were to be brought into the faith, as Gentiles, and have fellowship with Jewish believers on equal footing (Acts 15:7-11).

Therefore, when the Gentile believers are brought into the picture, the "newness" of the New Covenant and its distinction from Mosaic *torah* are as well. Fellowship under the *torah* of Moses is on the basis of *brit milah* (circumcision); without *brit milah* there could be no fellowship. The leadership of the New Covenant assembly determined that Gentiles were to be fully accepted without *brit milah* (Acts 15:1-31). They recognized that the identity of all believers would not be dependent upon the practices of the *torah* of Moses, but according to faith in Yeshua as expressed through a New Covenant orientation.

Thus Gentiles' inclusion in the body of Messiah and equality with Jewish believers reveals the evident need for a New Covenant, which would provide a new authority for faith and practice. Believers who claim to be submissive directly to the *torah* of Moses, and yet have fellowship and spiritual unity with uncircumcised Gentiles, are violating the very precept of the law of Moses to which they claim to be submitted.

Therefore, it would be incorrect to say that we are following the *torah* of Moses as our authority for faith and practice. Rather, under the *torah* of Messiah and in fidelity to the New Covenant, there is complete fellowship between the circumcision and uncircumcision.

Moreover, by the authority of the Messiah we are able to enjoy the *torah* of Moses. It's all profitable, but "New Covenant lenses" help us to see *Tanakh* more clearly, so we might fully profit and honor Messiah in all the word of God (1 Timothy 1:8-11). Therefore, New Covenant followers of Messiah "keep the feast," and set our yearly worship schedule with respect to Leviticus 23, because all these appointed times still proclaim Yeshua, even as the shadow does a body (1 Corinthians 5:7-8; 16:8; Colossians 2:16-17).

Even as Psalm 119 makes it clear that we have great cause to rejoice in God's word, through New Covenant *torah* one not only enjoys, but also applies Mosaic *torah*. For Jewish believers in Messiah, we are called to express our identity and faith as Jews in a manner that is relevant to our people (1 Corinthians 9:19-23). This is our New Covenant liberty, and is also our responsibility. Gentile believers as well have the same liberty to express their faith through New Covenant *torah* in a way that sensibly communicates who God is in Messiah. In the following chapter, we will further hone this relationship between the New Covenant faith and Mosaic *torah*.

Second: Miraculous Provision of Relationship with God

"And I will be their God, and they shall be My people" (Jeremiah 31:33b). This intimate work of God upon our souls results in relationship. The greatest assurance of the unchanged election of Israel is that the house of Israel "shall be my people"! The New Covenant Scriptures reiterate this in Romans 11:29, where Paul teaches that in regards to Israel, "the gifts and the calling of God are irrevocable." In the Hebrew text of Jeremiah 31:33, it is not the "I" that is emphasized, but the word "they." *They*, the very people that sinned and broke covenant with me, will be my people!

God didn't start all over with a new people, but made a New Covenant for his people! The point is simple and it is repeated throughout the word of God. Those who have sinned, those who have broken *torah*, those very people will recognize what God's grace alone can do. The truth of the whole word of God is that we are all here to prove His "grace alone as sufficient"—and that is done through our "weaknesses" (2 Corinthians 12:9).

In the end, it is not your sins that keep you from God. Oh, don't get me wrong; sins break relationship with God, and separate us from Him (Isaiah 59:1-2). But the sins of your life are not the final problem. Thank God, there is a cure for sin: "The blood of Yeshua cleanses us from all sin… if you confess your sins He is faithful and just to forgive you your sins and cleanse you from all unrighteousness" (1 John 1:7, 9).

Our real problem is when we do not address sin as sin, or foolishly think that God isn't all that holy, or that He's not all that concerned about sin. Then we will not recognize the cure. The New Covenant is for people who recognize the disaster that they have sinned and need forgiveness; those who realize that they have broken covenant with God and need His mercy and grace in Messiah.

The Mosaic *torah* was and is needed that we would understand that God is holy, and that "all have sinned and fallen short of His glory" (Romans 3:23). But only the New Covenant can now bridge the gap of sin and rightly relate us to God. We have some bad programming, and need a new program written on our hearts. Does your heart condemn you? "I'm a loser!" needs to be changed to "I can do all things through Messiah who strengthens me" and "I am more than a conqueror through Him who loved me" (Philippians 4:13; Romans 8:37).

What's written on you're heart? Some re-writing may be needed. Similarly, many individuals have bad marriage ideas taken from non-biblical sources. Thus when their relationship fails they just replace the spouse. But with the same bad marriage ideas in a brand new marriage, you will end up with the same problems all over again. Like a house built on a solid foundation, every marriage needs to be a New Covenant relationship that is unbreakable and permanent.

Third: Universal Provision of the Knowledge of God

> And they will not teach again, each man his neighbor and each man his brother, saying, "Know the Lord," for they will all know Me, from the least of them to the greatest of them. (Jeremiah 31:34)

Here the key phrase is "they will all know Me." God truly wants people to know Him. God created us in His image for this reason: to be in a relationship with Him. Of all God's creation we alone are designed to know Him, and to truly relate to Him. Then that which breaks God's heart will break our hearts as well.

A relationship with God is the fulfillment of your life and of God's will. He alone can fully understand your hurts as well. So what keeps us from enjoying God's provisions for our lives? Sin. What keeps people from knowing God? Sin. God cannot relate to, nor place His word in the heart of man, nor can man know Him, because of the separation of sin. This condition is made clear throughout the Scriptures:

> And those who handle *torah* did not know Me; For My people are foolish, they know Me not; My people are destroyed for lack of knowledge. (Jeremiah 2:8; 4:22; Hosea 4:6)

Some may wonder "I have my own religion. So, is 'knowing the Lord' all that important?" Yes, it's everything. Yeshua taught, "This is eternal life, that they may know You, and Yeshua the Messiah whom You have sent" (John 17:3).

No matter how religious or well behaved you may be, if you don't know the Lord, you do not have His life. In the New Covenant when you come to faith in Messiah, you are spiritually united with Yeshua by the Holy Spirit (Romans 6:5;

1 Corinthians 6:15-17). It is in this union with Messiah, this 'spiritual oneness' whereby we know the Lord and receive His eternal life.

How does a person come to know the Lord? When the truth of God is written on the heart, you don't need to be told to know the Lord – you will already know Him, personally. That's why the New Covenant Scriptures give this assurance:

> But you have an anointing from the Holy One, and you all know ... as for you, the anointing which you received from Him abides in you, and you have no need for anyone to teach you; but as His anointing teaches you about all things, and is true and is not a lie, and just as it has taught you, you abide in Him. (1 John 2:20, 27)

This is not ceremonial, but personal and intimate. Thus, coming to know the Lord is essentially experiential, not educational. A highway sign may say, "New York City," but it is not the actual city. In the same way, the teaching about Yeshua isn't the end in and of itself, but it directs us personally to Yeshua. Only by personal faith in *Him* can you know the Lord!

The best part of the Good News is this: the Lord loves everyone, and all who are willing can come to know Him! "All will know me," that is, all who have this New Covenant relationship, having experienced that internal work done by the Lord means you now know the Lord!

One day, the nation of Israel will turn to the Lord, making the prophesied national confession, "All we have gone astray, each one has turned to his own way; but the Lord has laid on Him the iniquity of us all" (Isaiah 53:6). When this is nationally fulfilled for Israel, it will be the national revival that both Zechariah and Paul prophesied about (Zechariah 12:10; Romans 11:25-27).

THE NEW COVENANT BRINGS FORGIVENESS OF SINS

Just how does the New Covenant brings about a personal relationship between God and covenant-breaking sinners? How can God remain a holy God and still accept wicked sinners?

"For I will forgive their iniquity" (Jeremiah 31:34). The reason that the New Covenant is Good News for covenant breakers is that only the New Covenant is actually 'keep-able.' This is because it is based on a fulfillment already accomplished in Yeshua's atonement. The New Covenant is established upon God's forgiveness for sinners, not on man's ability to keep laws.

At His last Passover meal before His death, Yeshua held up the third cup, the cup of redemption, and said, "This cup which is poured out for you is the New Covenant in My blood" (Luke 22:20). The New Covenant is established in Messiah's atonement for sins; therefore, there is forgiveness for sinners.

The *torah* of Moses demanded a holy righteousness of each person: "You shall be holy as the Lord your God is holy" (Leviticus 19:2). Messiah accomplishes this very righteousness for each of us who places our faith in Him, as Paul explains in Romans 10:4, "For Messiah is the goal of the Law for righteousness for all who believe," and in 2 Corinthians 5:21, "He that knew no sin became sin offering for us that we might become the righteousness of God in Him." Therefore, in light of His atonement, we are called "to proclaim forgiveness in His name" (Luke 24:46-47).

THE NEW COVENANT BRINGS FORGETFULNESS OF SINS

"And their sin I will remember no more" (Jeremiah 31:34). What is forgiven through the New Covenant is forgiven eternally. Consider the writer of Hebrews' interpretation of this passage:

For by one offering He has perfected for all time those who are sanctified. And the Holy Spirit also testifies to us; for after saying: "this is the covenant that I will make with them after those days, says the Lord: I will put My laws upon their heart, and on their mind I will write them," He then says, "and their sins and their lawless deeds I will remember no more." Now where there is forgiveness of these things, there is no longer any offering for sin. (Hebrews 10:14-18).

Messiah's atonement is final, sufficient, and so effective that God's forgiveness is once and for all time, and never needs any other sacrifice for sins. When Yeshua died on the cross and said "it is finished" (John 19:30), He meant finished… forever!

In Messiah, when you are forgiven, you are eternally forgiven, and what is forgiven through the New Covenant is eternally forgotten. God's forgiveness is so perfect, it is as if you had never sinned at all: there's nothing left to remember. The New Covenant orients our dependence on Yeshua, and not upon our own performance or obedience. When we sincerely repent and trust in Yeshua's death for our sins, God no longer remembers. The account is cleared, cleansed, and then filled with Messiah's own righteousness. When God forgives, He forgives completely; when He forgets, He forgets forever. If for one moment God were to remember our sins that He had previously forgiven, He would be denying the efficacy of His atonement in Yeshua!

Our enemy, Satan, the accuser of the brethren, is always glad to help us in either remembering the sins of others against us, or in dredging up our own past sins and the condemnation we feel as a result. In so doing, we don't experience the freedom and joy our relationship with God was intended to provide. To bring to mind what has been forgiven in Yeshua is to forget the fullness of forgiveness we have in Messiah. The New Covenant contains not only full acknowledgment of our sins, but also the full acceptance of our lives in the full atonement by our Lord. Through the New Covenant we can forgive and forget, too.

These three provisions promised in the New Covenant establish a vision for Messianic spiritual life, forever rooted in Jewish tradition, yet inclusive to Gentiles. In Messiah, the New Covenant has been inaugurated, and serves as the promised security for Israel and for all who believe on Yeshua.

Heaven and Earth will pass away, but My words will never pass away.
                            Matthew 24:28

13

MATURE FAITH

> "Do we then nullify the Law through faith?
> May it never be!"
> Romans 3:31

Many Jewish and Gentile believers in Messiah Yeshua are confused as to their relationship to the *torah* of Moses. Some teach that believers in Messiah Yeshua, especially Jewish believers, are still under the Law's authority for their fellowship, honor, and obedience. A more general problem is that Mosaic *torah* is often treated as largely irrelevant to the spiritual life of a believer. Other than a few Bible stories for children, it may be neglected from serious study and application.

Jewish believers always had the responsibility and liberty to keep Jewish practice faithfully, and they originally used it for the sake of testimony to Israel. Irenaeus was a disciple of Polycarp, the disciple of the apostle John. In about 180 CE he wrote a book entitled *Against Heresies*, to safeguard the faith delivered by the apostles, wherein he recorded this simple historical fact:

> And the Apostles who were with James allowed the Gentiles to act freely, yielding us up to the Spirit of God. But they

themselves, while knowing the same God, continued in the ancient observances... Thus did the Apostles, whom the Lord made witnesses of every action and of every doctrine... scrupulously act according to the dispensation of the Mosaic law... (Ante-Nicene Christian Library, Vol.5/1, Pp.313-314).

Yet, commenting on Deuteronomy 18:15, which speaks of Messiah, the Talmud says:

Come and hear: *Unto him ye shall hearken*, even if he tells you, 'Transgress any of all the commandments of the Torah' as in the case, for instance, of Elijah on Mount Carmel, obey him in every respect in accordance with the needs of the hour! (Yevamot 90b).

The rabbis are certainly not saying that the *torah* of Moses is done away with in Messiah, but rather that the true prophet has ultimate authority. The implication is that Messiah would be the prophet who would, like Moses and Elijah, perform miraculous signs and wonders, destroy the power of the oppressor, and redeem Israel. And, like Moses, He would present God's Law to the people. In the Dead Sea scrolls from Qumran, especially in the "Rule of the Community," Messiah is presented as the final interpreter of God's *torah* (e.g. 1QS 3.13; 4QFlor. 1:11-12). To some extent, this same role had also been anticipated in 1 Maccabees, concerning the cleansing of the altar which had been defiled (1 Maccabees 4:46).

Thus, *torah* was expected to change in the days of Messiah. The rabbinic Midrash on Psalms suggests that unclean animals may be declared clean:

Some say that in the time to come all the animals which are unclean in this world God will declare to be clean, as they were in days before Noah. And why did God forbid them? To see who would accept his bidding and who would not; but in the time to come he will permit all that He has forbidden (Midrash Tehillim 146:7).

The rabbis also considered that in the days of Messiah the children of forbidden marriages will be considered pure (Kiddushin 72b). Other rabbinic writings refer to a new *torah* that is related to the *torah* given at Sinai but different in some respects:

> The Holy One, blessed be He, will sit in Paradise and give instruction, and all the righteous will sit before him and all the hosts of Heaven will stand on his right and the sun, and stars on His left; and the Holy One, blessed be he, interprets to them the grounds of a new *torah* which the Holy One, blessed be He, will give to them by the hand of King Messiah (Yalqut Shimoni on Isaiah 26).

Thus, it is crucial from a Jewish perspective that we not seek to downplay the newness of *torah* in Messiah, and this perspective will help us understand the New Covenant better. In Romans 3, Paul first demonstrates that a person is saved by faith in God's salvation provided in Messiah Yeshua, and not by any works of the Law: "For we maintain that a man is justified by faith apart from works of the law" (Romans 3:28). Paul then seems to reinstate the relationship between faith and law: "Do we then make void the law through faith? Certainly not! On the contrary, we establish the law" (Romans 3:31).

Rather than the Law being made void, it is actually established by our faith. In fact, only faith in Yeshua establishes the eternal *torah* of Moses! But in what way does our faith establish the Law? And how is it that the Law is not voided when we are saved by faith "apart from works of the Law"?

FAITH ESTABLISHES THE LAW'S PARAMETERS

As stated, there are people who mistakenly think that believers in Messiah have, in effect, lowered the standard. That is, since the Mosaic *torah* was too difficult to keep, we simply found an easier way to God. Yet Yeshua taught the very opposite:

Do not think that I came to abolish the Law or the Prophets; I did not come to abolish but to fulfill. For truly I say to you, until heaven and earth pass away, not the smallest letter or stroke shall pass from the Law until all is accomplished. Whoever then annuls one of the least of these commandments, and teaches others to do the same, shall be called least in the kingdom of heaven; but whoever keeps and teaches them, he shall be called great in the kingdom of heaven. For I say to you that unless your righteousness surpasses that of the scribes and Pharisees, you will not enter the kingdom of heaven. (Matthew 5:17-20)

Anyone attempting to "lower the bar" of righteousness, by annulling even the least of the commandments, is both removing the standard that brings us to recognize our need for mercy, and also intimates that Yeshua's death was unnecessary.

The law, or works of the law, cannot save, and both justification and sanctification are by the grace of Messiah. The *torah* of Moses and the Good News of Messiah are not in conflict, since they both speak of God's righteousness. It is not freedom from Law that we desperately needed, but rather freedom from sin. The biblical teaching of "justification by faith" is the teaching of the *Tanakh* every bit as much as it is the New Covenant (Romans 1:17; 3:20-21; Habakkuk 2:4).

The word that Paul uses in the Greek for "make void" or "nullify" is *katargeo* (Romans 3:31). The basic sense of this word is to cause to be idle or useless. The term denotes a superior power coming in to replace the power previously in effect. For instance, light nullifies darkness. Darkness only exists where there is no light. Turn on the light and the darkness disappears. In the Septuagint, *katargeo* is used for the Hebrew word *betel* for "stop" or "cease," as in "stopping the work from continuing" (Ezra 4:21, 23; 5:5).

Paul is asking, "does our faith in Messiah and the New Covenant render the *torah* of Moses inoperative?" Though you may have been misinformed that the law of Moses is finished or no longer relevant, and thus might answer "yes," the answer here is a resounding "no!" Faith in Messiah does not nullify the Mosaic *torah*. Let's take a broad view: in a practical sense, grace does not nullify our responsibility to keep a job, care for our families, love our spouses, be faithful to our friends, be responsible Jews and Gentiles, and so on. Rather than annul these things, faith in Yeshua actually establishes us in our responsibilities, obligations, and commitments. Thus Paul states that our faith establishes the Law.

However, Paul also uses *katargeo* with respect to the Law in three other portions as well. There he indicates aspects of a believer's relationship to Mosaic *torah* which have been nullified.

THE LAW'S AUTHORITY IS NULLIFIED BY FAITH

Further in Romans, Paul writes, "the law has jurisdiction over a person as long as he lives" (Romans 7:1). The issue Paul is examining is the jurisdiction, or authority, of the *torah* of Moses over the life of a believer. Through death, the wife is released (*katargeo*) from the law to her husband (Romans 7:2). Just as a wife is under the jurisdiction of her husband while both of them are still alive, while we were "married" to the Law, we were under its jurisdiction and authority.

The rabbis pondered the relationship of the dead to *torah*, since the dead are to be resurrected with the coming of Messiah (Sotah 48b, Genesis Rabbah 96:5). Once a person has died, is he still obligated to observe all the laws? It was concluded that those who died were free from the commandments (Niddah 61b; cf. Shabbat 151b). However, freedom from the commandments, either through death or the resurrection, did not mean lawlessness or the freedom to disobey God. Rather, the rabbis believed that in the days of Messiah, "Man's deeds will be spontaneously good" (Leviticus Rabbah 18:1 n.5, citing Ecclesiastes 12:1).

195

However, this goodness comes, Paul went on to say, through dying to Mosaic *torah* so as to be joined to Messiah.

> Therefore, my brethren, you also were made to die to the Law through the body of Messiah, so that you might be joined to another, to Him who was raised from the dead, in order that we might bear fruit for God. For while we were in the flesh, the sinful passions, which were aroused by the Law, were at work in the members of our body to bear fruit for death. But now we have been released from the Law, having died to that by which we were bound, so that we serve in newness of the Spirit and not in oldness of the letter. (Romans 7:4-6)

Thus we are released from the authority of the Mosaic *torah*, and under the new jurisdiction and authority of our new Husband, Messiah! If we have died with Yeshua, the Mosaic law no longer has jurisdiction over our lives. Through our trust in and submission to Messiah we have a liberty of faith with respect to the Mosaic Law. Rather than being lawless, however, we are under the jurisdiction of New Covenant authority, or the "law of Messiah" (1 Corinthians 9:20-21). This authority in fact helps apply *Tanakh* to our lives.

Now, the New Covenant *torah* reveals the same holiness and priorities of God as does the Mosaic *torah*. Thus it is understandable how many are confused by the distinction between the two. When I lived in New York City, I could not legally make a right turn on a red light. But in North Carolina, it is legal to do so. Though there are mostly similarities between the driving laws of both states, the states themselves are distinct. When I moved from New York, I also left its jurisdiction and its restriction. Now I am under North Carolina jurisdiction and have the liberties and responsibilities of driving in this state. In a similar sense, the Mosaic law's jurisdictional authority over New Covenant believers has been nullified.

Again, to be clear, the witness, purpose, inspiration, applicability, and profitability of the Mosaic law has in no way ended, only its jurisdiction as law over believers. In Colossians 2:14, this same jurisdiction is called a "bond" or "certificate of debt," "having canceled out the certificate of debt consisting of decrees against us, which was hostile to us; and He has taken it out of the way, having nailed it to the cross." It is not only forgiveness of the debt, but a removal of the jurisdiction of the *torah* of Moses to ever put us under a moral debt again.

Therefore we can develop our first principle: Mature faith does not submit to Mosaic law apart from the New Covenant, but rather applies Mosaic law under the authority of New Covenant *torah* (Matthew 11:28-29; 1 Corinthians 9:20-21).

THE LAW'S GLORY IS NULLIFIED BY FAITH

The Mosaic *torah* came with a certain glory (*doxa*), the idea being of splendor or honor. Yet this glory in itself had limitations. 2 Corinthians 3 is Paul's *midrash* (comments and teaching) on Exodus 34:29-35. As mediators of a New Covenant, we live by the Spirit not by the letter. Here, Paul says that the glory Moses received in the Law was "fading" and "fades away" (*katargeo*).

> But if the ministry of death, in letters engraved on stones, came with glory, so that the sons of Israel could not look intently at the face of Moses because of the glory of his face, fading as it was, how will the ministry of the Spirit fail to be even more with glory? For if the ministry of condemnation has glory, much more does the ministry of righteousness abound in glory. For indeed what had glory, in this case has no glory because of the glory that surpasses it. For if that which fades away was with glory, much more that which remains is in glory. (2 Corinthians 3:7-11)

Since the Mosaic *torah* fulfills its purpose in showing us our great need for mercy and grace in Yeshua, it results in condemnation if we seek salvation and glory from it. That the glory upon the face of Moses was fading demonstrated the limited glory that could come from the Mosaic *torah*.

The New Covenant is thus "a ministry of righteousness," since we receive God's righteousness in Messiah. The glory that the Spirit gives through the New Covenant far surpasses the glory derived from the Mosaic *torah* (2 Corinthians 3:4-6). The Mosaic *torah* was the promise; the New Covenant *torah* was the fulfillment of the promise. The lasting glory of the Mosaic *torah* is Yeshua Himself. All of its other glory was to fade away, to be nullified, whereas Messiah and His glory is to remain forever.

> Therefore having such a hope, we use great boldness in our speech, and are not like Moses, who used to put a veil over his face so that the sons of Israel would not look intently at the end of what was fading away. (2 Corinthians 3:12-13)

Paul states that in light of the surpassing glory and honor that we have in the New Covenant, we are to be bold in our ministry, not like Moses who had to hide his fading glory. We proclaim the truth openly without veils. At first, Moses wore the veil in order not to blind those around him with God's glory (Exodus 34:29-35). But after a period of time the veil was to hide the fact that the glory was fading away.

> But their minds were hardened; for until this very day at the reading of the old covenant the same veil remains unremoved, because it is taken away in Messiah. (2 Corinthians 3:14)

As that veil prevented the Israelites from seeing the end of the fading glory, the *hardness* is like a veil over their minds at the reading of *torah*. Thus, they do not see how Messiah is the goal of the Law (Romans 10:4). This hardness upon Israel is *in part* even as it is also upon the Gentiles (Romans 11:25; Ephesians 4:18).

Even as Moses removed the veil when he came before the Lord in Exodus 34:34, the veil of hardness is actually "removed" (*katargeo*) by faith in Messiah Yeshua, who is the same Lord. The veil over our minds is replaced with the greater and lasting glory of the New Covenant (2 Corinthians 3:15-18). If we will look to Yeshua and receive His cleansing, acceptance in the family of God, and assurance of eternal salvation, we can live openly, transparently, honestly, 'without veils.' We do not need to try to gain glory, honor or a sense of self-worth by keeping the Mosaic *torah*. By the finished work of Messiah we are brought into relationship with God, and receive honor and our sense of identity through the ministry of righteousness in the Spirit. In Messiah we have the certainty of His glory (Romans 8:29-30).

We therefore can develop a second principle from this section: Mature faith does not glory in the Mosaic *torah*, but has confidence through Messiah's New Covenant. Our boast is in Yeshua alone (1 Corinthians 1:30-31), who applies *torah* to our hearts.

THE LAW'S HOSTILITY IS NULLIFIED BY FAITH

The final aspect regards relationships between Jews and Gentiles. We considered this already in chapter 10, and can briefly revisit it. The Mosaic *torah* directed Israel to live in such an observant way that they would be separated in lifestyle as well as in beliefs from the nations, and their pagan, sinful customs. Again in Ephesians, Paul uses the word *katargeo*, where it is translated "abolishing," to describe the enmity which existed between the two groups:

> For He Himself is our peace, who made both groups into one and broke down the barrier of the dividing wall, by abolishing in His flesh the enmity, which is the Law of commandments contained in ordinances, so that in Himself He might make the two into one new man, thus establishing peace, and might reconcile them both in one body to God through the cross, by it having put to death the enmity. (Ephesians 2:14-16)

The enmity produced by the Mosaic *torah* is nullified in regards to believers. There are no second-class believers in Yeshua. If we have been accepted by grace, we are to accept one another graciously, as well. We therefore can develop our third principle: Mature faith does not segregate or exclude other believers on the basis of the Law, but has unity with all believers in Messiah.

To summarize, from these sections we see that though faith does not nullify the Law, the Law's authority, glory, and enmity, with respect to followers of Messiah, are, in fact, nullified (authority, Romans 7:1-6; glory, 2 Corinthians 3:7-12; enmity, Ephesians 2:14-16). We see three principles from these truths for those of mature faith. Though the New Covenant does supercede in those aspects, it does not nullify the purpose of the Law of Moses. As noted above, the confirmation of the *torah* by the Good News means that the truth of justification by faith is the teaching of *Tanakh*, as well as the New Covenant. This is also largely consistent with traditional Jewish teaching about the days of Messiah. Mature faith not only establishes the Law, but also lives in the liberty, certainty, and unity, provided graciously in Messiah Yeshua.

FREEDOM FROM LEGALISM

Yes, I am aware that there are Messianic believers who teach submission to the authority of the Mosaic *torah*, glory in it, or even uphold a separation. They are my brothers and sisters in Messiah. Lowell Thomas related a story of two privates in the Fifteenth Infantry, who had been ordered to make their way to a bridge, and guard it:

> Private Glenn Sollie and Private Bearshield were faithful soldiers. They went and they guarded and guarded. They stuck to it for three days and three nights without food and without blankets. Then they were—no, not relieved, they were found. They were guarding the wrong bridge. The two brave warriors had lost their way and taken their battle stations at a bridge seven miles away from the one they were to guard. They might still be there, if the Fifteenth Infantry had not sent out a detail to look for them (*Pageant of Life*, 200).

Messianic believers who believe we are under Mosaic *torah* seek to be faithful—but they are guarding the wrong bridge. The truth of the Good News of Yeshua is the bridge that leads home, and it is the bridge we are called to guard. However, whereas one may be confused by making Mosaic *torah* the focus (which thus takes away from the focus of *torah* itself), this needs to be distinguished from a greater spiritual danger. We call this danger "legalism." This is the more general notion of believing, practicing, and teaching that the mere keeping rules or laws will make you, or keep you, right with God. Perpetrators of such teaching may be, in fact, as Messiah said in Matthew 7:15, "wolves in sheep's clothing," looking to steal away His children. Of these Paul wrote,

> I know that after my departure savage wolves will come in among you, not sparing the flock; and from among your own selves men will arise, speaking perverse things, to draw away the disciples after them. (Acts 20:29-30)

Though they use words to appear as actual believers, their beliefs are wrong, and they desire to enslave you in their own legalistic bondage. Yeshua was harder on the religious legalists of His day than the irreligious prostitutes and tax collectors. So was Paul, and we should be as well.

Legalism is "more general" because the rules one puts above Messiah may be from places besides Mosaic law. Some legalists may insist on *kashrut*, worshipping on Shabbat, or keeping other parts of Torah as meritorious for achieving righteousness with God. Less rare, however, are New Covenant legalists, those who believe that you must contradict *torah* since you are free in Messiah. They might spy out our liberty, shocked that we do not eat a pork chop! They may insist that Sunday is now mandatory Shabbat, or say that the resurrection must be celebrated with Easter, and certainly not to be identified with Passover.

Such New Covenant legalists have worked contrary to the Scriptures, contrary to the plan of God, and in effect hide the Good News from the eyes of the Jewish people. This is not to be condoned. These legalists would put you into their own form of bondage, thinking it "Christianity." When witnesses of a so-called Good News assert that for a Jew to believe in Jesus, the Messiah of Israel, they should abandon their Jewish heritage, this is wicked legalism. Many such groups in reality have a different Jesus, a different Spirit, and a different Gospel!

To rebut the claim that real believers must come under any legal system to be made righteous before God, Paul says "listen to the Law!" In so doing he places their disagreement in the historical context of Mosaic *torah* itself (Genesis 21:8-14; Galatians 4:21). Paul says in Galatians 4:4-5,

> But when the fullness of the time came, God sent forth His Son, born of a woman, born under Law, so that He might redeem those who were under Law, that we might receive the adoption as sons.

Messiah born under this good system redeemed those of us born under that same system. Do you wish to be under that system? If so, then listen to it and learn. Mosaic *torah* does not teach you to be under law, but points in a different direction—to cling to Messiah and the promise fulfilled in Him. To think that we are to place ourselves under mere rules and regulations rather than under Messiah is neither the teaching of the New Covenant nor the Mosaic *torah*.

> It was for freedom that Messiah set us free; therefore keep standing firm and do not be subject again to a yoke of slavery. (Galatians 5:1)

We are free according to God's promise. God's grace, the power of the Holy Spirit and truth of God's word will make us more than conquerors in Messiah, and able to honor God in all our ways. So be resolute in the pardon of Messiah, and turn away from trusting in mere regulations.

Messiah made it clear:

"You shall love the LORD your God with all your heart, and with all your soul, and with all your mind." This is the great and foremost commandment. The second is like it, "You shall love your neighbor as yourself." (Matthew 22:37-39)

Thus, *torah* comes full circle, making application of the original instructions to Moses, by the inspired words of Messiah Himself. May God help us to yield our lives completely to Him, and to learn to truly care for others. May we find rest in our Lord, and proclaim the Good News of Messiah's triumphant work in His death and resurrection. Faith in Yeshua, His love, sacrifice and grace, is the true bridge to Heaven, and the key to living a heavenly life here on Earth!

SELECTED BIBLIOGRAPHY

Arnold Fruchtenbaum, *Israelology*
Dan Gruber, *Copernicus and the Jews*
Dan Juster, *Jewish Roots*
Barney Kasdan, *God's Appointed Times*
David Stern, *Jewish New Testament Commentary*

OTHER BOOKS BY SAM

Messiah in the Feasts of Israel - this book shows how the Feasts supernaturally and biblically point to Messiah.

Even You Can Share The Jewish Messiah - A short booklet with key information on sharing Yeshua with friends and neighbors, even "to the Jew first" (Romans 1:16).

The Messianic Answer Book - Answers to the 15 most asked questions Jewish people have about the faith. Excellent tool for sharing with those seeking answers.

Messianic Wisdom: Practical Scriptural Answers for Your Life - Get a grasp on Messianic Jewish issues and living out your faith in Messiah. Essential and inspiring, this book is for every growing disciple of Yeshua.

The Messianic Passover Haggadah - The perfect guide for conducting your own Passover Seder.

Messianic Discipleship: Following Yeshua, Growing in Messiah - leads the reader through a Jewish discipleship course, treating the essentials of Messianic faith.

Messianic Life Lessons from the Book of Ruth - an in-depth, information-rich devotional commentary on what is a priceless book of restoration from the Tanakh.

Messianic Life Lessons from the Book of Jonah: Finding and Following the Will of God - Do you want to know God's will for your life? Jonah proves this will not help! A slender, wonderful commentary on this book about Israel's mission to the Gentiles.

SCRIPTURE INDEX

Genesis
1:5	180
1:27	167
1:28	18
2:16-17	167
3	18
3:1	47
3:7	167
3:15	45
5:24	160
9:9	167
9:16	151
12	45
12-14	44
12:1	155
12:1-2	87
12:2	37, 41, 156
12:2-3	129
12:2-3	130
12:3	28, 81, 87, 156, 161
12:7	87, 155
13:14-17	155
13:16	156
15	43
15	45
15-21	44
15:5	44, 45, 87
15:6	44, 45, 46, 47, 55, 56
17:4	156
17:5-9	129
17:7	151
18:25	61
21:8-14	202
22-25	44
22:16-18	49
22:17-18	156
22:18	87, 156
24:2-9	77
26:5	167
35:11	41
46:28	166
48:19	116-117
49:1	130

Exodus
12:48	78, 182
12:49	166
15:4	166
16:28	166
16:30	178
16:4	166
19	153
19:5-6	153
19:6	92
22:31	171
23:19	171
29:31-33	176
30:29	98
31:12-13	178
31:16	151
32	157
32:13	155
32:14	155
32:9-10	154
34:14	83
34:29-35	197
34:29-35	198
34:34	198

Leviticus
4:20	138
6:18	98
7:15	138
11	175
11:44-45	171
16	158
17:11	66
18:24	139
19:2	40, 52, 58, 187
19:15	59
22:32	32
23	176, 183
23:10-12	97
23:29	63
24:8	151
25:27	50
25:5	50
25:52	50
27:18	50
27:23	50

Numbers
15:20-21	97

Deuteronomy
4:30	12
4:37	16
7:3	77
7:6	25, 98
7:6-8	13
7:8-9	26
8:11-18	70
9:6	26
10:15	16
10:16	168
14:21	171
18:15	192
23:1	160
23:5	16
24:1-4	168
28	153
28:1-2	153
28:13	97, 104
28:15	154, 156
28:16-68	154
28:62	156
28:63-65	155
29-30	150, 155
29:1	155
29:24-27	155
29:24-28	156
29:4	155
29:4	156
30	156
30:3-5	156
30:6	150, 156, 165, 168

Scripture Index

30:9	156	**Psalms**		11:9	93
30:16	157	5:5	71	14:12-14	70
32:43	130	9:8	61	24:5	151, 157
Joshua		14:1	22	26	193
1:9	40	14:2	64	27:9	118, 119
23:6-7	139	15	70	28:16	144
Ruth		18:49	130	29:7-8	12
1:16-17	90	32:1	50	33:14-15	70
4:13ff	99	32:2	50	40-66	204
1 Samuel		34:2	71	40:9	20
20:8	15	51:18	120	45:25	52
24	100	76:2	144	49:22	118
26	100	78:1	166	49:8	58
2 Samuel		78:10	167	53	31, 37, 41, 204-205
5:7	120	78:68	17	53:10-11	67
7:12-14	159	80:8-9	96	53:11	52
22:5	130	89:28	15	53:4	50
23:5	151	105:10	151	53:6	64, 187
1 Kings		110:1-2	159	55:3	151
6:23-33	95	110:4	159	56:3-7	160
8:39	144	117:1	130	57:19	142
10:9	16	118:22	144	59:1-2	64, 119, 137, 184
14:31	99	119	183	59:20-21	118-120
2 Kings		137:5	36	60:1-6	87
7:9	20	145:17	51	61:8	151
1 Chronicles		**Proverbs**		63:16	73
16:17	151	1:8	166	65:2	13
2 Chronicles		4:2	166	65:17-18	161
2:11	17	13:14	166	66:12	118
36:21	178	16:18	102	**Jeremiah**	
Ezra		31:26	166	2:8	185
2:2	164	**Ecclesiastes**		4:2	156
4:21	194	12:1	195	4:4	168
4:23	194	**Song of Songs**		4:22	185
5:5	194	2:15	173	9:23-24	71
6:17	164	**Isaiah**		11:16	96
8:35	164	2:1-5	92	23:5-6	158
Job		2:3	87, 120	23:6	59
29:20	151	4:2	158	30:2	12
		5:1-7	96	30:3	164
		7:15-16	60	30:7	11, 164
		9:6	138	30:8	12
		11:1	130	30:16	12
				30:24	12

30:24-31:1	164	11:1	17	12:12	179
31:1	11-12	14:4	17	15:24	129
31:1-3	123	14:6	96	15:26	15
31:27	164			16:18	37
31:29	164	**Jonah**		18:20	40
31:3	11-16	2:10	70	19:10	169
31:31	150-151, 157, 164	3:9	158	19:11	169
				19:26	43
31:31-34	121, 140, 149-188, 157	**Micah**		19:3	167
		4:1-4	92	19:3-11	167
		6:8	70	19:6	168
31:31-37	78	7:16-17	97, 104	19:8-9	168
31:32	152	7:20	17	19:9	168
31:32	167	**Habakkuk**		22:37-39	203
31:33	157, 158, 163-184	2:4	70, 194	24:15-34	12
				24:32-34	96
31:33b	183-184	**Zechariah**		25:4	12
31:34	158, 165, 185, 187	1:8	96	26:28	165
		2:11	118	28:1	179
31:35-37	34, 37, 129	3:1-3	12	28:18	39
32:40	151	3:8	158	28:18-20	39
50:5	151	6:12-13	159	28:19	39, 175
		6:12-14	158	28:20	40, 142
Ezekiel		9:1	164		
16:60	151	12:10	12, 52, 156, 187	**Mark**	
20:20	178			6:5	20
26:26-27	161	13:1	52, 121	7:21	166
28:12-19	70	13:9	164	11:12-14	96
36:26	165	14:16	12	11:13-14	97
36:26-27	150			11:20	97
37:1-14	93	**Matthew**		16:2	179
37:1-14	116	5:17-18	152	16:9	179
37:23-27	164	5:17-20	194		
37:26	151	5:28	166	**Luke**	
		5:28-29	169	1:35	20
Daniel		5:32	168	2:36	164
1	174	6:10	93	5:17	20
12:2	93	6:13	120	6:19	20
		6:21	166	12:47-48	61
Hosea		6:33	99	15:16-17	11
3:1	17	6:9	32	15:20	123
3:5	12, 156	7:15	201	19:41	13
4:6	185	10:5	15	20:17	144
6:7	166	11:28	142	21:24	116
9:1	96	11:28-29	178, 197	22:20	151, 165, 187
9:2	96	12:7	179		
10:10	96	12:8	179	22:7-8	101

207

23:56	178	13:14-15	89		194
24:1	179	13:46	26	1:18	54, 58, 122, 141
24:46-47	187	13:46	27		
24:46-48	142	14:1	27, 27	1:19-20	124
24:46-49	144	15	77	1:20	124
		15	160	1:21	82
John		15:1	77	1:28-30	169
1:16	113	15:1-31	182	2:4	103
3:16	13, 14, 15, 83	15:5	77	2:9-10	24, 28
		15:7-11	182	2:11	99
3:17-18	54	15:10	101	3	193
3:36	54, 60, 156	15:14-18	116	3-5	62
5:9-11	179	15:20	176	3:2	24
7:37	142	15:20-21	177	3:20	58
7:37-38	126	15:29	176	3:20-21	194
8:24	119	16:1-3	77	3:21	45, 58, 71, 73, 161
8:56	67	16:1-3	181		
8:58	45	16:13	178	3:21-22	71
10:23-25	119	17:2	178	3:21-31	57
15:1	96	17:17	89	3:22-23	59, 63
15:1-6	96	18:4	178	3:23	22, 64, 134, 142, 184
15:5	134	20	180		
15:13-15	49	20:6	101, 112, 179	3:24	65
17:3	186			3:25	66
19:30	188	20:7	179, 179-180	3:25-26	54, 66
20:1	179			3:27-28	69
20:19	179	20:16	101, 180	3:28	72, 193
20:21	131	20:20	89	3:29	72
		20:29-30	201	3:29-30	72
Acts		21:11-13	87	3:3	73, 93
1:8	21, 142	21:21-24	171	3:31	191, 193-194
2:46	177	21:25	176		
3:12-26	25	22:3	40	4	28, 45
3:19 21	85	22:28	135	4:3	45
3:25-26	25	22:28	135	4:11-12	47
4:12	73	23:5	100	4:22	46
8:1	124	26:7	164	4:23-25	46
8:5	124			5:1	53, 54, 138, 141
10	25	**Romans**			
10-11	134	1:2	28	5:6-8	13
10:13-14	175	1:3	28	5:10	122
10:28	175	1:4	21	5:12	114
11:1-3	77	1:5	48	5:12-19	51
11:3	182	1:16	19-31, 205	5:12-21	28
11:26	84	1:16-17	19, 28	6-8	62
12:19	124	1:17	23, 28, 30, 52, 70, 70,	6:5	186
13:14	178			6:11	56

Scripture Index

7:1	195	11:11-15	77-93	11:31	28, 124, 131, 136
7:1-6	176, 200	11:11-24	79, 80, 109		
7:2	195	11:11-31	14	11:36	126
7:4-6	196	11:11-32	79	12-15	62
7:12	58	11:12	84-86, 91, 113, 115, 116, 117	12:2	151
7:18	22			14-15	174
8:3	91			14:1-3	174
8:4	167	11:13	27, 28, 88	14:1-12	127
8:17-22	93	11:13-14	86-91, 112	14-15:7	128
8:29	62	11:14	88, 90	14:13-16	174
8:29-30	199	11:15	85	14:13-23	127
8:37	21, 185	11:15	91-93, 97, 111, 113, 115	14:17	174, 177
9:1-4	27			15:1	130
9:3-4	86			15:1-3	174
9:3	110	11:16	97-98, 100	15:1-6	127
9:3b-4	122	11:16-24	95-107	15:3-4	128
9:4	123	11:16-25	80	15:5-6	128
9:4-5	96, 123, 129	11:17	98-100	15:7	127-128
9:6	110	11:17-18	111	15:8	15, 98, 128-130, 131
9:23	84	11:17-24	85		
9:31-10:4	23	11:18	80, 100-101	15:8-12	128
9:32-33	80	11:19	101-102	15:8-13	128
10:1	14, 23, 34, 89	11:20-21	102	15:9	26, 130
		11:22	81, 103	15:9-12	130-131
10:2	54	11:22-24	103	15:11	130
10:4	45, 105, 152, 187, 198	11:23	55, 103	15:12	130
		11:24	103, 104-107	15:25-27	87
				16:25	110
10:6-9	156	11:25	84, 85, 109-118, 198	16:25-26	156
10:12	84			16:26	48
10:21	13	11:25-26	110		
10:21	123	11:25-27	187	**1 Corinthians**	
11	55, 78, 95	11:25-29	80	1:18	20
11:1	27, 28, 79, 86	11:25-32	109	1:30-31	199
		11:26	12, 34, 90, 97, 114, 120	1:31	71
11:1-10	79-80, 82			2:1-5	21
11:1-2	26, 37, 92, 111			5:7-8	183
		11:26-27	118	5:8	182
11:1-6	14	11:28	98	6:14	21
11:2	41	11:28a	124	6:15-17	186
11:2-4	79	11:28b	124	6:9-10	169
11:5	110	11:28-29	121, 129	6:9-11	124
11:5-6	79	11:29	93, 123, 184	7:10-13	168
11:7	85	11:30	124	7:18	181
11:11	28, 80-84, 112, 113, 131, 136	11:30-31	85	7:18	182
		11:30-31	114	8	177
		11:30-32	80, 123	8:7-12	177

209

Scripture Index

8:8	176	6:1	90	2:14b-15a	138-139
8:13	172, 177	6:2	58	2:15	161
9	177	12:9	21, 22, 184	2:15b-16	140
9:19	89	13:4	21	2:17	137
9:19-20	38			2:17-18	142
9:19-23	183	**Galatians**		2:19	136, 142, 143
9:20-21	196	2:7	87		
9:20-21	197	2:11-12	175	2:20	143, 144
9:20-22	88	2:11-14	182	2:20-22	143
9:21	167	3:1-5	46	2:21	144
9:22	90	3:11	70	3:1-13	133
9:23	89	3:14	87, 130, 155	3:4-9	110
10	177	3:17	77	3:6	138
10:5-11	170	3:19-24	176	3:7	21
10:26	113	3:22	125	3:14-21	133
11:25	151	3:22-24	71	4:4	141
11:30	170	3:24	161	4:18	198
13:5	56	3:6	45, 47	4:23	151
14:24-25	144	3:6-9	47	5:32	110
15:1-4	20	4:4-5	202		
15:2	93	4:16	86	**Philippians**	
15:20-23	8	4:21	202	2:5-8	91
16:1-4	180	4:26	121	3:2	135
16:2	179	5:1	202	3:10	21
16:2	180	5:6	141	3:11	93
16:3	87	6:12	167	4:6-7	138
16:8	183	6:15	161	4:7	14
				4:13	185
2 Corinthians		**Ephesians**			
3	197	1:7	66, 84	**Colossians**	
3:4-6	198	1:9-10	110	1:13	24, 120
3:5-6	158	1:14	133	1:26-27	110
3:6	151	1:19	20, 59	1:27	84
3:7-11	197	2:1-10	133	1:29	21
3:7-12	200	2:5	82	2:2	110
3:12-13	198	2:7	84	2:9	113
3:14	198	2:7	103	2:9-10	84
3:14	199	2:8-10	48	2:9-17	174
4:7	21	2:11-12	134	2:10	141
4:16	151	2:11-22	133	2:11-13	165
5:14	14	2:12	137	2:13	82
5:16	73	2:12-13	15	2:14	197
5:17	161	2:12-13	41	2:16	174
5:18-20	92	2:13	137	2:16-17	183
5:21	53	2:14	140	2:17	174
5:21	138	2:14-15a	137	2:21-22	176
5:21	187	2:14-16	199-200	4:3	110

1 Thessalonians
1:1 120, 121
4:16-5:5 115

2 Thessalonians
2:3-12 12
2:7 110

1 Timothy
1:8-11 183
3:6 70
3:9 110
3:16 49, 110, 173
4:1-5 172, 176
4:3 173
4:4 173

2 Timothy
1:8 20
3:11 120
3:15-17 152
4:16 50
4:18 120

Titus
2:3-5 206

Philemon
1:18-19 51

Hebrews
2:10 65
3:14 138
3:19 114
4:6-11 114
4:9 178
7:11-14 159
7:12 159-160
7:25 160
8:13 151
8:8 151
9:9-10 175
9:15 151
9:15 151
10:10 173
10:14-18 188
10:25 178
10:38 70
11:1 51
11:5 160
11:6 100
11:8 45
11:19 49
11:27 160
11:32 99
12:22 121
12:22-24 165
13:2 151
13:9 176

Jacob (James)
1:1 164
2:10-11 160
2:22 49
2:23 45, 48-49
4:4 143
5:20 170

1 Peter
1:5 20
1:15 40
1:15 167
2:2 99
2:6 144
2:9 176
2:11 143
3:7 59

2 Peter
1:16 20
3:9 120
3:16 171

1 John
1:7 120, 184, 169
1:9 120, 169, 184
2:15 143
2:16 70
2:20 186
2:23 61
2:27 186

2 John
9 23, 60

Revelation
1:10 179
1:20 110
2:5 170
2:14 176
2:16 170
2:20 176
2:22 170
3:3 170
3:12 121
7:4 113
14:6 151
20:8 113
21:1-2 161
21:2-3 145
22:20 93

Other Writings

Apocrypha
1 Maccabees 4:46, 192

Mishnah
Sanhedrin 10:1, 118

Talmud (*Bavli*)
Berachot 25a, 171
Shabbat 15b, 139
Shabbat 89a, 140
Shabbat 151b, 195
Ta'anith 8a, 21
Yevamot 63a, 99
Yevamot 90b, 192
Sotah 5b, 21
Sotah 48b, 195
Kiddushin 72b, 193
Sanhedrin 98a, 119
Makkot 23b, 71
Avodah Zarah 4a, 21
Avodah Zarah 28, 95
Niddah 61b, 195

Midrash
Genesis Rabbah 96:5, 195
Exodus Rabbah 36:1, 95
Leviticus Rabbah 1:2, 99
Leviticus Rabbah 18:1 n5, 195
Tehillim Rabbah 146:7, 192

211

For more information, please contact us at:

WORD OF MESSIAH MINISTRIES
P.O. BOX 79238
CHARLOTTE, NC
28271, USA

PHONE: (704) 544-1948

WORD OF MESSIAH MINISTRIES

Visit our website at:
www.WordofMessiah.org

"Messianic Foundations"
by Sam Nadler
Copyright © 2010 by Sam Nadler
Word of Messiah Ministries
All rights reserved.
Printed in the United States of America

ISBN-13: 978-1534877771

ISBN-10: 1534877771

Made in the USA
Columbia, SC
14 January 2022